utopian entrepreneur
Brenda Laurel

Designer
Denise Gonzales Crisp

Editorial Director
Peter Lunenfeld

MEDIAWORK   The MIT Press Cambridge and London

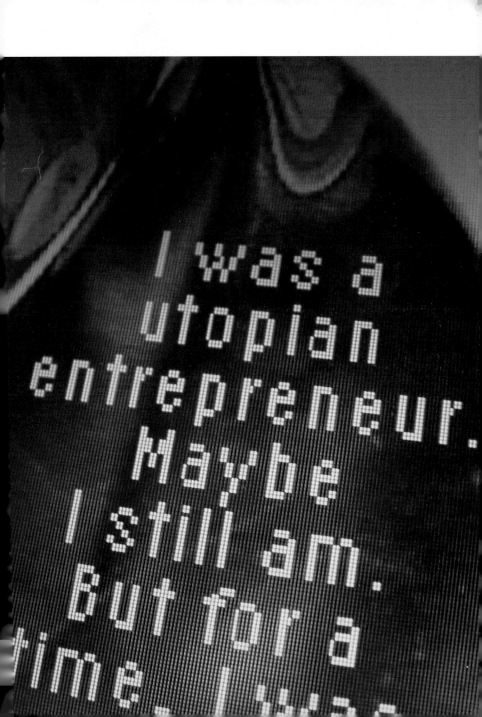

, I was also

Cmdr. B. Laurel, a Navy test pilot, and I rode a modified F-14 into the desert floor. I've made the 60,000-foot downward spiral in some of the F-4 Phantoms and F-18s of the computer game industry—Atari, the old Activision, Epyx. This last time it felt different—I think I was fonder of the plane. My F-14 was Purple Moon, a company I co-founded, which was devoted to making interactive media for little girls. It was a dream come true.

The ironic thing about this flameout was that I got into doing games for girls precisely because I was so tired of seeing things explode.

The players in the drama of Purple Moon were diverse— earnest

researchers,

nerdy

RICH GUYS,

lesbian separatist designers,

businesswomen with

BARRACUDA SMILES,

strident feminist reporters,

Barbie,

Rockett,
and several million
little girls. At Purple Moon we played with various structures

for interactive narrative and tried to do positive work for girls in the context of popular culture. I took a lot of heat from some people who call themselves feminists for portraying girl characters who cared about such things as appearance, popularity, belonging, betrayal, and all the other *sturm und drang* of preadolescent friendship. *Some people thought I shouldn't do that because girls shouldn't behave in this way. But they do, you see. And who* they become depends a great deal on how they manage their transit through the narrows of girlhood.

As a parent of girls, what you hope for most is that they discover their own personal power at this moment in their lives. Our heroine, Rockett Movado, was unique in her ability to see the possibilities open to her and to make conscious choices about what to do next. Our products allowed girls to try this skill and to see how things might turn out differently depending on what moods, attitudes, or choices they brought into the next moment.

Six and a half years and $40 million later, we had interviewed thousands of kids, invented a narrative world and a diverse cast of characters, published eight CD-ROM games, produced a wildly successful Website, and built and lost a company. The girls' games movement, launched in 1996 by *Barbie Fashion Designer*, stimulated a retail feeding frenzy and generated hundreds of millions of dollars in revenues. In its three-year life, Purple Moon claimed the high moral ground, offering diversity, personal relevance, and respect for girls as its central values. But the company's destiny was nasty: it rocketed from a spectacular launch to sudden bankruptcy, finally to be gobbled up for a bargain-basement price.

rockett's wake.
After the company closed down, we had a wake for Rockett at my house. Each of us spoke, and as founder, I delivered the final eulogy. Rockett's little plastic body was laid out on an antique table in my living room in her own miniature locker. Black candles, bouquets of purple irises, and a seriously depleted bottle of Irish Whisky flanked the casket. I poured a shot for myself and one for Rockett in a plastic medicine cup that had belonged to one of my daughters. "We're always trying to heal something—lousy childhoods, raw deals, crappy self-esteem. We were trying to heal something when we made her." I lifted my glass and the roomful of former Purple Moon employees followed suit.

"To the little redheaded girl." I toasted the medicine cup.

Everyone applauded. On cue, my daughters stepped up to the table, and like pallbearers took up the tiny coffin and marched it solemnly upstairs. The evening's toasting and storytelling had already been leading to tears, and now people wept openly as the little body passed.

"This circle is open but unbroken," I concluded. Right on cue,

THE MIRACLE OCCURRED.

ROCKETT DESCENDED

slowly from above,
transformed.
Her lavender sweater
and backpack
were hidden beneath a billowy, hot-pink gown.

Hot-pink-feathered angel wings fluttered as she was lowered on a piece of pink yarn by giggling girls on the landing. A cheer rose from the assembled artists, writers, animators, producers, marketeers, and kids. We couldn't tell them yet that Rockett was going to join Barbie in the afterlife, but it seemed a little foreshadowing was in order. Otherwise, I was afraid, the shock would kill them. Two weeks after the wake, and a month after Purple Moon was closed down by its investors, and we all lost our jobs, Mattel announced that they would acquire the company's characters and properties.

Nobody made a dime.

Here's one of the perversities of dot-capitalism: if Purple Moon had not actually produced any real products, I'd probably be "post-economic" today. Just as the dot-economy started spinning straw into gold, Purple Moon was spending real money to make real products to go onto real shelves in real stores. In investment terms, that was a big mistake. Even though we had an extremely popular Website, the embarrassing detail of real goods prevented us from passing for a dot-company in the venture community. And so, instead of the wild valuations that made some of our younger friends multimillionaires, the valuation of Purple Moon could never exceed some small multiple of our revenues—because we actually had revenues.

Because Purple Moon did not make it to the big IPO or a lavish acquisition, it would be understandable to conclude that the methods I'll advocate here don't work: no million-unit titles, just respectable sales in a new market segment that got crowded really fast. Our eight CD-ROMs and our Website won all kinds of awards but didn't make us profitable in time to satisfy our investors. *There are other measures of success, however, and I think things can be learned from our experience.*

The coffin—with Rockett still in it—is in the top of my closet now. My little girls have become teenagers, spinning slowly away into their grown-up lives. Through teaching and writing and time, I think I've just about recovered from the Purple Moon adventure. I've done quite a few interesting consulting gigs since Rockett went upstairs, but none of the consumerist crap that passes for the "Industry" these days has tempted me to make another passionate, all-consuming commitment. Not yet. This little redheaded girl is now a middle-aged veteran of Silicon Valley. I've learned some chops, and I'm looking for the next worthwhile opportunity to use them.

culture work

The saga of Purple Moon is not simply a business narrative of economic success or failure. It is the story of how a group of writers, designers, programmers, artists, and marketeers got funding from a Microsoft billionaire to become culture workers. *Purple Moon was the crucible that forged my new outlook on the responsibilities of creative individuals to their cultures.* It made me think that in the twenty-first century, design innovators must also become economic innovators; that a "new economy" that doesn't confront issues of politics and ethics is as "old" as child labor and poorhouses; that we can do better than always placing public benefit in opposition to private gain.

I'm not unaware that combining "utopian"

In the competitive world of business, entrepreneurship produces winners and losers; utopianism strives for a world where everyone succeeds and harmony abounds. America's recent burst of economic prosperity has institutionalized a shortsighted selfishness. At the same time that government institutions devoted to promoting public welfare face criticism and decreased funding, businesses gain little or no advantage either by contributing to the public good or by refraining from causing public harm. When forces opposed to taxation and regulation triumph, both government and business are released from accountability. Utopian entrepreneurs manifest a different ethic simply through the force of their choices and actions. They insist that the practices and outcomes of the businesses they build be harmonious with the public good, even when it's perfectly legal and often more profitable to do otherwise.

Thus far in my career, I've been at the wave front of four major paradigm shifts. In 1977, I got involved in the embryonic personal computer business, designing interactive fairy tales for the Cybervision system—a personal computer with 2K of usable RAM. At Atari in the early 1980s, I was part of the first big boom of the computer game industry. In the late 80s, I co-founded a company devoted to the budding field of virtual reality. Through Interval and Purple Moon, I participated in the evolution of the Web economy in the 1990s.

Along the way, I've learned that our steps always falter in the wake of a great new idea, especially one that captures the collective imagination. In all the excitement, people develop extravagant expectations which are bound to be thwarted in the short term. A really powerful medium—such as movies or videogames or virtual reality—also spawns exaggerated public fears. When neither hope nor fear is realized, the public becomes disillusioned. This phenomenon reminds me of how our feelings change as our children pass from youthful innocence into "troubled" adolescence.

Personal computers floundered until Apple brought the desktop metaphor into the mainstream.

Computer games looked like they were all over when Atari crashed, until Nintendo and a new generation of personal computer games began to fill the void with innovation. Virtual reality failed to deliver the equally desired and dreaded hyperreal immersion in worlds of fantasy; today it delivers value in areas as diverse as archeological reconstruction and mineral prospecting. The initial economic models that drove the Web crashed and burned with the NASDAQ in 2000. Oh, we thought, that's the end of that. But of course, it never is. New paradigms continue to be explored by people who poke at the edges; the public responds by reframing hopes and expectations; and the character of a new medium begins to emerge. The process of maturation in new media requires creativity, time, investment, optimism, and freedom—exactly those things a skeptical society is in no mood to grant.

For nearly twenty-five years in games and interactive media, my goals have been focused on injecting humanistic values into the content and culture of computer-based media. I have been in excellent company. *People who believe in this new utopianism share a simple optimism: we think we can make a difference.*

We don't think *Fahrenheit 451* is a done deal.

In their critiques of contemporary media, some politicians and moral leaders would have us continue to take things off the table, especially away from young people. No more violent videogames, no more R-rated movies. But these culture police seem to forget that when the movie industry attempts to attract the lucrative teen audience through any means, it is just doing what prevailing business ethics prescribe: make money, period. There is no business value in social responsibility; it will not raise your stock price or increase your revenues. Instead of dealing with the problem productively, our leaders are content to "just say no."

The young today are well acquainted with having things taken away.

In fact, if we measure freedom in terms of the ability to move safely around in the world or to think independently, they have less freedom than ever before. Saying no again—this time to movies and games that provide the illusion of personal power through violence—is more likely to lead to classroom shootings and suicides than so-called violent media. The answer for our kids and our culture is not "no" as a default response. Socially responsible people must take up the challenge of creating games and movies and stories that both engage and nurture young people. Yes, socially positive creators are held to a higher standard.

To find a compelling substitute for violence

IS HARD.
TO MAKE A
BUSINESS
SUCCESS OF IT
IS HARD.

BUT THESE THINGS
ARE
POSSIBLE
AND
NECESSARY.
A UTOPIAN ENTREPRENEUR
IS ONE WHO STEPS UP

TO SUCH CHALLENGES.

Popular culture shaped me. As a child of the 50s, I was an avid audience for television, movies, books, and music. My earliest heroes were Perry Mason and Davey Crockett. I watched Westerns and read Nancy Drew mysteries. As I grew, my values were influenced by *Star Trek*, *Kung Fu*, fantasy and science fiction (especially J.R.R. Tolkien, Ray Bradbury and Arthur C. Clarke), films like *Fantasia* and *Twelve Angry Men*, novels like *To Kill a Mockingbird*, and all of the books of Alan Watts. The music of the Beatles,

Laura Nyro, and Crosby, Stills, and Nash was woven into the fabric of my identity. As the culture turned in the late 60s, Woodstock and the psychedelic movement took center stage. Call it boomer nostalgia if you will, but I feel very fortunate that I came of age during a time when positive, humanistic values were so richly reflected in pop culture.

My experience gives me faith in the power of popular culture to shape values and inform citizenship, influencing both public and private institutions. When I got involved in the embryonic computer game business, I recognized that it could be one of the wellsprings of a new pop culture. This was around the time when *Star Wars* and *Close Encounters* were released and *Roots* was broadcast on television. I admired people like George Lucas, Alex Haley, Ursula K. Le Guin, Toni Morrison, and even Stan Lee for offering powerful images of honor and ethical behavior.

It took me many more years to discover that I couldn't effectively influence the construction of pop culture until

I stopped describing myself as

(a) an artist, and
(b) a political activist.

Both of these self-definitions resulted in what I now see as my own self-marginalization. I couldn't label myself as a subversive or a member of the elite. I had to mentally place myself and my values at the center, not at the margin. I had to understand that what I was about was not critiquing but manifesting.

Working with popular culture can be dismaying if you're looking for depth and significance. Philosophical, political, and spiritual matters are seen to be central to the discourses of the arts and humanities, not the material of popular culture. In America, there's long been a schism between art and popular culture. Too many artists circumscribe their audiences by restricting themselves to a kind of peer-to-peer philosophical dialogue, conducted exclusively in the academy and the gallery. The argument for this elitist practice is that the general public has been too dumbed down by popular culture to understand higher-level discourse. But maybe the converse is true—perhaps the public doesn't understand the philosophical dialogue because no one is making art for them.

When artists and philosophers talk only amongst themselves, they ignore the potential of popular culture to become a variety of dialogues with and between everyday people. Its discourse may be productive of desire and pleasure, but popular culture is also a language in which people discuss politics, religion, ethics, and action. Many creative people feel they must choose between the art world and popular culture, and people who see the general public as their audience may no longer be considered artists by their peers. I no longer call myself an artist.

I think that culture work is A MORE APPROPRIATE DESCRIPTION OF what I do.

I am committed to working in the language of popular culture. Doing culture work well requires research. Our work relies on our understanding of perception, cognition, and how people construct meaning. Culture work also functions as research. We are continually informed about our time and our nature through the responses of people to the artifacts of popular culture.

Humanists who attempt culture work will always be attacked by elites who claim their political turf and insist that people doing values-driven work must by definition be marginalized. The vogue for cultural studies notwithstanding, there are still plenty of folks who believe popular culture is intrinsically poisonous. If it is popular, it is bad for you; if it is bad for you, it is probably popular. There is a great deal of inevitability about it. If you do market research, you are probably fundamentally crass and exploitive. This position is possible because the values at the heart of humanism still have not been understood. CULTURE WORK EXCITES THE WILL TO ACTION.

It requires means of dissemination, often found in commercial media, which after all are at the intersection of communication technologies and the market economy.

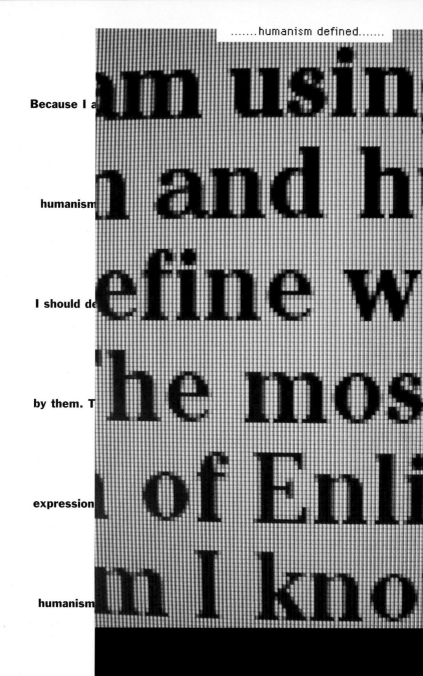

Because I a

humanism

I should de

by them. T

expression

humanism

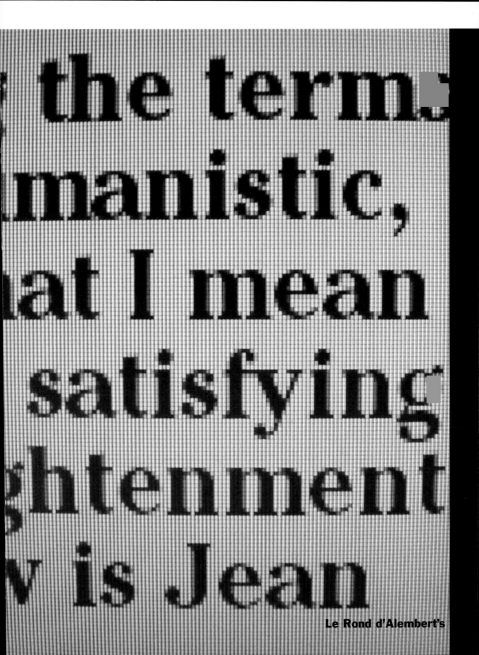

the term:
manistic,
at I mean
satisfying
ghtenment
v is Jean

Le Rond d'Alembert's

Preliminary Discourse to the Encyclopedia of Diderot. D'Alembert describes the principal aims of the encyclopedia, to "set forth as well as possible the order and connection of the parts of human knowledge," and "to contain the general principles that form the basis of each science and each art." D'Alembert believed we might continually improve the human condition through our own efforts. While believing in the primacy of sensation and observation as how we know the world, the Encyclopedists advocated a methodology that submitted these observations to reason, and, sometimes not so obviously, to ethical consideration.

The truth is that humanistic work is values-driven work. It is work you are doing because you think it's a good thing to do. Enlightenment humanists fell at different points on the continuum between universal truths—including ethical values—and empirical investigation. So do humanists today. Many will deny they have values and claim their work is entirely objective. But this is to ignore the shining single value that is the very heart of humanism:

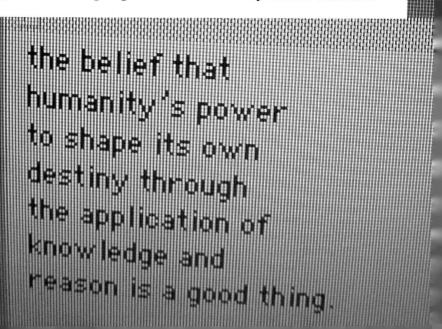

the belief that humanity's power to shape its own destiny through the application of knowledge and reason is a good thing.

In other words, whether we admit it or not,

humanists make the implicit assumption that we can **do** good,

and therefore that we can know what is good to **do**.

I realize invoking the Enlightenment at the dawn of the twenty-first century may strike some as just a bit retro. Enlightenment values such as Reason were mangled in attempts to justify appalling acts of repression, and science has, after all, enabled humans to create technologies of mass destruction. For fifty years, then, we've dutifully engaged in a critique of the Enlightenment and its legacy.

Yet, as rigorous as the process may have been, the whole appartus of critical/postmodern/cultural studies discourse never managed to excite me into action in the same way those original, if bruised, ideals did. I return to

humanistic values, which for all their misinterpretations and misapplications, validate humanity's ability to create a better **future**, and which offer both an ethical ground and a methodology for setting about it.

People living in the world today are experiencing a bewildering rate of change and complexification. Because we are all in this together, culture workers have these ethical goals: to help people to adapt, to retain their integrity, and to flourish under conditions of profound change. The strategy of culture work is to inject new material into the culture without activating its immune system. That new material coalesces around age-old questions: What is the meaning of this? Who am I? What are the world and I becoming?

purple moon.

Throughout my two decades in the computer game business, I had ached for a chance to create alternatives to the chasing, shooting, fighting, exploding, hyper-male world of games. Why weren't there any computer games for girls? And why did I end up losing my job every time I suggested it? It couldn't be just a sexist conspiracy. The boys' game business generated billions of dollars; surely even the most virulent sexist in Silicon Valley would be perfectly happy to reap the corresponding billions from girls if he could figure out how to do it. Nor was the male culture of computer games simply an artifact of the history of the industry. Something more complex and subtle was going on, and I knew it had to do with the construction of gender embedded in every aspect of our lives—in play, identity, work, technology, and business.

In 1992 I met David Liddle, who was just forming Interval Research Corporation with his partner, Paul Allen, the cofounder of Microsoft. Bulging with brains and flush with Allen's $100 million initial investment, Interval was indisputably the hottest new gig in Silicon Valley. Allen was bored with desktops and PCs; he envisioned a lab that could deliver a paradigm shift. He wanted Interval to invent a new industry for him to play in. Liddle wanted PARC without the Xerox hanging off of it. Both men suspected that the next best technologies would be invented,

not for the workplace, but for people at home and in public spaces.
So Interval was destined to explore popular culture.

As he built the research staff, Liddle hired a brilliant mix of
forty-somethings and smart young inventors fresh out of school.
The gender balance—at least 30/70—was something of which
he could be very proud. The resulting culture was a lovely blend
of techno-euphoria and social idealism. Later, that idealism
would become problematic for Liddle. He didn't want the lab
or its projects to look dreamy-eyed or impractical to Allen or other
potential investors. One of the ways in which he over-compensated,
I think, was to dismiss the Web as something only for geeky enthusiasts—
a technology he predicted would never enter the mainstream.

When we first met, Liddle had read my book *Computers as Theatre*
(1991), and I had read about the work he directed at Xerox PARC, the innovative laboratory that had pioneered everything from the graphical user
interface to the Ethernet. Over dinner that evening, we discovered we had
a strong common interest. Both of us were curious as to why there didn't
seem to be any computer games for little girls. We both knew exposure
to computer games gave boys a level of comfort and familiarity with the
machine that girls generally did not share. Neither of us knew of any reason
why girls would be intrinsically less interested than boys in computers or
computer games, and both of us were deeply puzzled as to why no one had
been able to make something that worked for them. Liddle's summary of
the missed business opportunity was: "There's a six billion dollar business
with an empty lot next door." Most important, we agreed if this were an
easy problem, someone would have already solved it. In sum, it had all the
characteristics of a good research problem

—puzzling, consequential, and complex.

I didn't just want to study the problem,
I wanted to do something about it.
Interval gave me that opportunity.

I actually met with **Paul Allen** only once.
He was generally preoccupied with building his
portfolio in cable and wireless, taking time out to bask
in the celebrity glow of his enormous and enormously
public investment in Dreamworks SKG (the movie
studio whose oft forgotten initials stand for Spielberg,
Katzenberg, and Geffen). Most of Paul's business got
done by his diminutive blond investment prodigy,
Bill Savoy. Paul appeared occasionally at Interval's
summer picnics, sitting in on bass with the company's
favorite band, D'Cuckoo. He played really well, and
his face got all relaxed and spacey in that way
musicians have. My husband and I always danced to
his playing, but we never spoke with him. Notoriously
shy, he always avoided eye contact.

When we were about two years into
the research on gender and technology, David set up a
meeting for me to pitch the project to Paul for
continued funding. Paul looked casually natty in a light
blue oxford shirt, khakis, and

those Docksider boat shoes. He still wouldn't meet my gaze. He was sitting in a little conference room next to his business development guy, Verne Rayburn. Middle-aged and chipper, Verne exuded competence and good cheer. His pink Polo shirt amplified the effect.

I handed out a neat outline of the research plan and enthusiastically drew pictures of the interface for the prototype we were hoping to build on the white board. I felt David pacing behind me as I faced the men across the table. Before the meeting, David had confided that he was worried Paul would think we'd made a politically motivated choice in hiring a female-dominated design firm—clearly an oddity in the game business—but he was ready to defend it if he had to. Verne seemed fascinated by the research and asked lots of the usual questions about girls' interests and play styles. I explained the embryonic concept of the Rockett series— days in the life of a new girl in eighth grade. Then Verne asked a question I didn't expect.

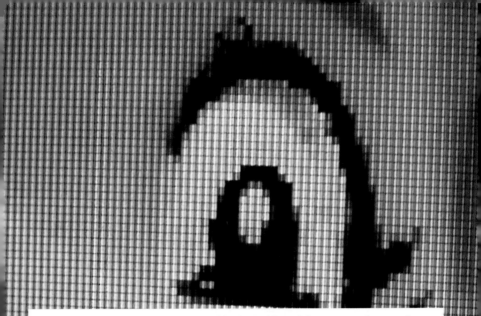

"Are we sure this isn't biased in terms of sexual preference? I mean, are we discriminating?" Paul stirred. David stopped in mid-pace. I groped for a reply, uncertain of what weird turf we had just stumbled onto. Verne didn't strike me as a social activist. I frantically began combing through our research in my mind to answer his question. "Truth is, it's not coming up for most girls this age. They're mostly focused on their relationships with other girls. I mean, peer relationships," I fumbled. "They talk about boyfriends, but they're pretty virtual. Sexual preference isn't an issue yet. And we're not focusing on boys or dating in the games we're hoping to—"

David jumped at the chance to turn a potential liability into a feature. "We've tried to be sensitive to that concern, Verne," he interrupted. "In fact, the development house we're working with has a fair number of lesbians."

The L-word ricocheted around the walls of the little conference room. There was a brief silence. Paul's head bobbed a little, then he returned to contemplating the tabletop.

Everyone had theories, but no one seemed able to back them up with good data or scientific evidence. I disagreed loudly and often about what had led to male domination of the world of computer games, but we agreed to let research settle the argument. The underlying conviction was that it would benefit girls enormously to achieve familiarity and ease with technology, and I suspected the most effective way to bring make girls comfortable with computers was through play. So I signed on at Interval and began a four-year research project, which led to the formation of Purple Moon.

I had worked for some of the most powerful companies in the game business, but until 1992, games for girls weren't even a twinkle in anyone's eye. Traditional marketing wisdom in the industry held that girls weren't a viable segment. In fact, they wouldn't even constitute a niche market. Everyone knew girls simply didn't like computer games and wouldn't play them. Examples would be trotted out as proof.

My favorite was *Barbie*, published in 1985 by Epyx for the Commodore-64. Barbie was at the mall,

shopping for the right outfit to wear on her date with Ken.

Now, *"everyone knows" that girls aren't good at shooting games,* so the designers reasoned that the game should make it easier for them.

The brilliant solution: make projectiles that move slowly.

And so it was decided that

the action component of the game
WOULD CONSIST OF THROWING MARSHMALLOWS.

"You see," the game execs would say, "they did everything right, but sales were dismal." Therefore you can't sell computer games to girls. *Post hoc, ergo propter hoc.*

Our first goal at Interval was to articulate the research question. It seemed too narrow and trivial to ask simply, "Why hasn't anyone made successful computer games for little girls?"

This question has some ready-made answers. Computer games as we know them were invented by young men around the time of the invention of graphical displays. They were enjoyed by young men, and young men soon made a very profitable business of them, dovetailing with the existing pinball business. Arcade computer games were sold into male-gendered spaces, and when home computer game consoles were invented, they were sold through male-oriented consumer electronics channels to more young men. The whole industry consolidated very quickly around a young male demographic—all the way from the game-play design to the arcade environment to the retail world—and it made no sense for a company to swim against the tide in all three of these areas at once. And that's just the obvious stuff.

Given all these barriers, who knew if girls and women would play computer games or not? Were there intrinsic gender differences that caused females to be repelled by computer games? How should we understand the exceptions—games that attracted a higher than usual percentage of female players, like *Mario Brothers*, *Tetris*, and *Myst*?

What would it take to design a computer game a large number of girls really liked?

Even though the occasional computer game like *Pac Man* was a hit with girls and women, scoring sometimes as many as twenty-five percent female players, conventional wisdom remained fundamentally unchallenged. Whenever a girl title was attempted, it was launched all alone onto the shelf without adequate marketing or retail support, and the inevitable failure became another proof that girls would not play computer games. As late as 1994, Sega decided to steer clear of the potential girls' market because they feared being seen as doing things for girls would alienate their male audiences. By the way, our research showed that—initially at least—their fears were indeed well-founded.

We spent several months consolidating our findings and then transforming them into design principles to use in developing products for pre-teen girls. I hired veteran Apple interface designer and fine artist Kristee Rosendahl to help us apply what we had learned to the design of merchandise and Web development. *Teen* magazine maven Pamela Dell, who introduced herself to me on email, eventually joined up as lead writer and invented Rockett and her friends. After a stage of advance development inside of Interval, we formed a company and launched three interconnected businesses—interactive CD-ROMS, the purple-moon.com Website, and an array of Purple Moon collectibles. We were emphatic about defining the company not by its products but rather by the people it was meant to serve. Purple Moon was a girls' company.

We launched our first products—two CD-ROM games and the Website—in 1997. Our first two Friendship Adventures, *Rockett's New School* and *Secret Paths in the Forest*, were both in *PC Data's* top 50 entertainment titles during the holiday season (right up there with *John Madden Football*) with sales at approximately ten times our original forecast. From launch until February 1999, the Website served over 300 million pages, with about 240 thousand registered users who visited us at least once a day and viewed an average of thirty-five pages per visit. These girls collected about five million virtual treasures and sent each other nearly ten million Web-based postcards. Over the life of the company we launched seven more CD-ROM titles, including more Friendship Adventures, creativity products, and the first-ever line of sports games for girls.

Throughout its life Purple Moon maintained a strong, ongoing

commitment to research.

.......with friends like these.......

Our crucial first Christmas sell-in exceeded our expectations, and the ample press coverage was 95% positive. Nevertheless, we received a crushing review from a middle-aged guy in the *New York Times* who asserted that he didn't need to let little girls play with them because he knew a bad game when he saw one. His piece got reprinted without a by-line in Silicon Valley's most important paper, the *San Jose Mercury News*, with the headline "This Rockett's a Dud."

Meanwhile, we were in the crosshairs of radical feminist Rebecca Eisenberg, who wore pink chiffon with combat boots and wrote for the *San Francisco Chronicle*. Rebecca's strident accusations of gender crimes were eventually reprinted by *Ms. Magazine*. Feminists were confused; is it good or bad to reflect the social realities of most girls' lives?

Although the vast majority of press was great, the negative reviews cut us to the quick, because they often came from those we were thought would be our natural allies. We were wrong, it was said, to bring up such issues as popularity. Girls shouldn't think about this, and so we shouldn't encourage them. After talking to thousands of girls and seeing survey results from thousands more, I say, "horsefeathers." Popularity is a pervasive concern for preadolescents. Emotional health is not about whether preteens think about popularity, but how they think about it and what kinds of values they employ in deciding how to behave.

A utopian entrepreneur will likely encounter unexpected criticism —even denunciations— from those whom she might have assumed to be on her side.

By trying to do anything socially positive at all, the utopian entrepreneur opens herself up to the endless critique that she is in fact not doing enough. For example, those few feminists who vehemently attacked Purple Moon games raised no objection to other contemporary girls' games that seemed much more heinous, like the appearance-obsessive *Cosmopolitan Makeover* or the remarkable bimbosity (to coin a word) of *Clueless*. I am reminded of the old saw: the one who attacks you is likely to be the one closest to you on the road. Here's some dialogue from a game about Rockett's struggle to decide whether to join a clique:

Darnetta: [giving advice to Rockett] Because they think this thing about you is cool, they want to be your friend because of it. But if they find out the thing isn't exactly true, they won't be down with you?

Rockett: That's right. That's totally my problem. So what should I do?

Darnetta: Rockett, you don't need friends like that.

I wondered, did anyone notice that this wasn't Barbie?—that Rockett struggled mightily to be ethical and self-defined? The answer is, YES—girls noticed. And many of their parents did, too. After the company's demise we received hundreds of letters thanking us for our work. It seems that everyone I meet at conferences or public events knows a girl who still plays Purple Moon. Even my youngest daughter sometimes dusts off her copy of *Secret Paths to the Sea* and

solves a puzzle for the hundredth time because she needs the wisdom and emotional balm of the story she knows she will find at the end of the path.

Our characters exhibited

loyalty,
honor,
love, and courage.

They also struggled with

gossip,

jealousy,

cheating,

lipstick,

smoking,

exclusion,

racism,

poverty,

materialism,

and broken homes.

When we had to choose, we sacrificed political correctness in order to meet girls where they were, in the realities of their own lives. Girls' responses over the years have made me certain that it was the right thing to do.

I consider our work to have been a cultural success in the sense that it touched the lives of millions of girls and offered them fresh views of girlhood and a new portal into the technology. But our business failed. It failed for reasons having to do with investors' expectations, market conditions, and some weakness in strategic planning. A few choices made differently would have made Purple Moon a financial success.

I have learned a great deal, and
I'm not dead yet.

When Purple Moon had its plug pulled by its investors—only six days after we had shipped our eighth CD-ROM title—we determined that we would need to close our Website. Even though the hosting bills were paid through the end of the month, the intellectual property was in legal limbo, and more seriously, with no operating company, there would be no one to watch the safety alerts and keep our promise to girls to make the site a safe place. So, with much sadness and beating of breast, we scrambled to create the semblance of a graceful ending in the midst of our corporate catastrophe. We put together a farewell screen on which our characters told the girls it was time to say goodbye. There was a cartoon portrait of the Web team created in *Rockett's Adventure Maker*, and I posted a message to the girls about how things don't always go the way we want, but we have to learn from our mistakes and carry on with honor and keep a positive attitude, etc. etc.,

stiff upper lip.

I was bombarded with email sent to my personal address, which would have required some Web-searching, from girls and parents dismayed at the closing of the company and the site. I found myself explaining bank-rupt-cy to 10-year-olds, trying to help girls get their hands on merchandise they needed to complete their collections, and struggling to comfort heartbroken girls who lost their online friends when the site closed down. Most of them had followed the practice of not giving out personal information to people you meet online, so the only connection they had with Purple Moon postcard pals was on the site itself. All of us were devastated that there hadn't been time to warn girls so they could figure out another way to connect with friends they had made.

Somehow Nancy Deyo, Purple Moon's dauntless CEO, finagled the funds to re-open the site temporarily, to give girls a chance to reconnect with their friends. That's when we noticed the miracle. During the nine days that the site was down, it had acquired 274 new registered users. It turns out that the program was still running behind the farewell screen. Girls who had bookmarks inside the site could get in, and most of the girls who were using it didn't know that there was anything unusual going on. The only way new users could have registered would have been that their friends helped them sign up from the inside, where we had cleverly installed a button labeled, "Want to let a friend sign on? Click here." Once the site reopened, the number of new registered users quickly regained its pre-shutdown level of about 400 girls per day.

THE INTERESTING THING HERE IS THAT THIS HAPPENED WITHOUT A PENNY IN MARKETING EXPENDITURES. IT WAS AS THOUGH

THE DEAD ROSE UP AND WALKED.

.......risk = reward.......

Culture workers are often marginalized for having humanistic goals. **But the folks who succeed in doing good in the world tend to be extraordinarily tough-minded.** If you have the knowledge and self-discipline to apply appropriate values to complex, interrelated tasks; if you have the commitment to pursue socially positive ideals through strenuously realistic means; if you have the chutzpah to promote change at the level of popular culture; then you are a hell of a lot more valuable than any self-indulgent "creative" or dot-com carpetbagger.

When Purple Moon was being formed, David Liddle explained to me that the amount of equity I could hope for would follow this simple business creed:

Liddle reasoned that multibillionaire Paul Allen was taking the big risk, having put several million dollars into the research and the fledgling company so far. Next to that risk, Liddle explained, my own was miniscule. The three and one-half years I had spent doing the foundational research, design, and project management had been well compensated by my salary, as would be my involvement in the new company. I was not putting millions of dollars at risk—only my hopes and dreams, my health, and my professional reputation. That risk was worth between one and two percent of the initial equity, which would, over the company's lifespan, be diluted by a factor of ten. When the company was finally shut down by its investors, that equity was worth nothing.

The risks and the rewards of utopian entrepreneurship are different from those of business as usual. You may be the creative wellspring of a new enterprise, you may give it all your passion and all your effort, and you may be absolutely essential to its existence, but unless you have a lot of money to put into the pot, your risk will probably not be seen as deserving of a large financial reward. Nevertheless, your rewards in terms of personal satisfaction, recognition, and influence may be large. Paul Allen is not known as the person who tried to buck decades of sexism in the computer game industry. Paul Allen is not known as the founder of Purple Moon. I am. And that is worth quite a lot. If humanist action in a commercial context is ever seen as the risk it truly is, utopian entrepreneurs may be better compensated economically as well. But in the meantime, there may be no reward as sweet as the hum of a studio working well, or mail from people who truly love what you've made for them.

research as practice. The Purple Moon experience

proved to me beyond any doubt that you have to talk to people, not just to see if they like your idea, but to find out what's going on with them, what their issues and tastes are, how they actually spend their time. I don't mean self-validating focus groups—I mean learning about people with your eyes and ears and mind and heart wide open. Such research does not necessarily require massive resources, but it does require a good deal of work and a concerted effort to keep one's assumptions in check.

I think one of the main reasons why the videogame business has been so horribly stunted in its growth is that it has been unwilling to look beyond itself to its audience. I can't count the number of times I've listened to middle-aged male executives hold forth on who boys are and what they want. These are guys who remember when Eisenhower was president. At best, they are living in the 50s; at worst, they are living in 50s-style denial of the fact that boys' lives today are radically different—and perhaps even more culturally impoverished—than their own boyhoods were. To be fair, I've heard women—Mattel executives and others—speak with equal confidence about what girls are like, based at best on their own experiences growing up in a different time, and at worst on the perennial gender stereotypes that are reinforced by the great machine of consumerism.

When I advocate research,
I'm not talking about
what we typically call
market research.

MARKET RESEARCH, AS IT IS USUALLY PRACTICED, IS PROBLEMATIC

for a couple of reasons. Asking people to choose their favorites from among all the things that already exist doesn't necessarily support innovation; it maps the territory but may not help you plot a new trajectory. On the other hand, most people are not very good at inventing new objects of desire. If you had asked someone in 1957 what new thing they would like to play with, chances are they would not have asked for a plastic hoop that they could rotate around their hips. Somebody had to invent the Hula Hoop®.

Well then, you say, the point is to find good, frisky inventors.

Who needs a bunch of pencil-heads in white coats asking questions?

Innovation is for the creatives. But no one in their right mind would suggest that research is a replacement for creativity. Research does you no good if you don't empower creative people to invent novel, cool things. Doing research and paying attention to your findings can simply better the odds of
success by illuminating the space of possibility and
focusing creative
energies.

When current models fail, what sense does it make to pull the plug on innovation? Research has fallen on bad times. With the closing of Interval, the breakup that left AT&T Labs an orphan, and the "for sale" sign on Xerox PARC, the uncertainty in other labs large and small, one wonders how long it will take for big companies to realize that it really is important to think more than six months out. Here's a common habit of industries in transition: when the models start to fail, the first funding cuts hit the researchers, creatives, and far-out thinkers. It's an automatic reflex. At the other end of the continuum, companies who find themselves with reliable cash-generating products tend to cut research budgets as well. As Liddle puts it: "You have to feed the bulldog"—that is, keeping a successful business growing usually requires that you feed it more and more resources.

But short-changing research always turns out to have been the wrong idea.

In an oft-quoted adage, research superstar and computer pioneer Alan Kay has said: "The best way to predict the future is to invent it." Given the current climate, we probably won't be able to depend upon corporate research to invent a very interesting future—at least not for several years. Many large companies, including HP, Microsoft, and Intel, are increasingly deploying research dollars as venture capital rather than funding large, long-term projects in the lab. The problem with venture funding as research, of course, is its

fundamental short-sightedness.
And who will fund the kind of long-term research

that will spawn new industries? How do you justify the expense of projects that may only pay off in the long run? What's the business plan, as they say in Silicon Valley?

A few wealthy foundations and a handful of hyper-rich beneficiaries of the computer industry's success have the resources to fund long-term research labs that are free of the blinders and fickle funding habits of established corporations. Bill Gates, Larry Ellison, John Chambers, and yes, Paul Allen—any of these people and a few others like them could take the lessons we learned from Interval and **build a lab that really works as an incubator, not just for new products, but for new industries.** Interval was, after all, a very good idea, and an extremely instructive failure. One lesson from Interval is to have a strategy for earning revenue from intellectual property that you don't choose to develop. Another is that a flat organization is inadequate to the needs of diverse projects—there wasn't enough management to go around. Among the most valuable lessons Interval offered is the importance of staying the course. Interval came under pressure to shift the focus of its business to emitting spin-offs before it was geared up to do a good job of it.

Spinning off companies requires a strong, up-to-speed midwifing capability, including a staff of experienced start-up business people and long-term working relationships with potential investors. As Liddle well knew and often declared, "apartment cats" don't survive well in the wild. Nevertheless, most Interval start-ups became mired in seemingly endless, essentially in-house negotiations with Paul Allen's Vulcan Ventures rather than toughening up through real-world encounters with the investment community. New companies are strengthened by real-world competition for funding. Investors can also help new companies find good operating officers—great researchers do not often make good executives. Most crucial is the seasoned, relevant business expertise investors can contribute to a newborn company's board and operating plan.

The team I managed at Interval was extremely fortunate to partner with Cheskin Research. I learned from Cheskin's methodology that it's not enough to understand people statistically—you need to find out what their lives are really like. Some of that is quantitative information, such as how much TV they watch or how often they play videogames. Some of it is qualitative: what makes them insecure or how they represent themselves to other people. Some of what you need to know may be scientific—for example, how good are people at pattern-matching, and how do their vision and reflexes change with aging? Some things are better gotten at through personal conversations and stories—what are your favorite things to do? Or, what magical powers would you like to have? These sorts of questions aren't particularly useful if the answers are multiple-choice—you can't learn much from "none of the above."

When I talk about Purple Moon research, people always want to know what we found out. It's pretty hard to summarize findings of such scope and variety. In terms of computer games, girls didn't mind violence so much as they disliked the lack of good stories and characters.

Regarding computers themselves, girls were much more likely than boys to blame themselves rather than the machine when things went wrong.

Did computer games discriminate against girls? The answer is probably yes. Science has produced provocative evidence that girls perform less well than boys at tasks involving mental rotation under time pressure, for example, and that they tend to prefer more body-centric navigational methods than boys, relying more on landmarks for cues. If these things are true, then featureless mazes and the left-to-right scrolling of traditional videogames have privileged male players.

And we haven't even touched on games' social content yet.

Social differences are more complex and difficult to quantify. Through a variety of methods, we satisfied ourselves that there are real differences in how American preteen boys and girls organize themselves socially. The status hierarchy for boys tends to be based on explicit factors such as strength, speed, and skill at some tasks. Competition among boys tends likewise to be fairly explicit. By contrast, a girl's social status among her peers is likely to be influenced more by her network of affiliations than by any explicit measure. Covert tools such as exclusion and secrets are prominent means of social competition. This is one of the "ugly" observations that so upset feminist critics of our work. But it seemed to us that acknowledging these tendencies and using narrative to explore alternative ways of expressing and dealing with them was healthier for girls than denying their existence.

One of my hobbies is reading about animal behaviors. Among chimps and other non-human primates, some similar gender differences in social organization can be observed. When journalists came to call at Purple Moon, our PR person always swept the primate books off of my shelves and hid them, afraid that fundamentalists might take offense. But it's obvious that much remains to be learned about human social behavior by observing our nearest genetic relatives.

GOOD RESEARCH IS NEVER DONE.

Some things about people may remain constant throughout life—a love of music, for example, or a propensity for orderliness. But other aspects of people are changing all the time, as a result of aging, experience, and the changes in their cultural and personal contexts. When we started Purple Moon, for example, girls' interest in team sports was just beginning to gather momentum. Girls' sports heroes were most likely to be figure skaters or gymnasts. Then the WNBA happened, and the U. S. women's soccer team captured the World Cup. We charted these changes in attitudes about sports and explored the experience of playing from a girls' perspective. Our ongoing research enabled us to design *The Starfire Soccer Challenge*— our pioneering sports game just for girls.

The first trick is to define your   1.
research goal appropriately.

The second trick is to expend the   2.
greatest energy
going deep,
even if
your
samples
are
small.

Trick   3.
number
three is
transforming what you find out
into design principles
you can actually use.

The fourth trick   4.
is to pay attention
to what you learned, even if
it doesn't match your personal taste
or the prevailing truisms about
your audience.

- If your goal begins with the words, "To prove that," then you have already foreseen your conclusion and biased your results. Recast the goal so that it begins with the words, "To find out."

- Ethnographic work, field observations, and in-depth interviews will yield insights you could never achieve through quantitative data alone. If you are studying an identifiable group of people, see their movies, listen to their music, and hang out in places they enjoy. Observe carefully and make notes. In the Purple Moon studies, Cheskin taught us the innovative technique of the "photo audit"—kids were given disposable cameras to photograph aspects of their lives. These pictures gave us priceless views into the private worlds and experiences of our audience. Large-scale quantitative studies may best be used as brackets; at the outset they can help guide you in choosing specific research directions, and in the final stages of research they can lend validity to qualitative findings. Look at published research— the numbers you need might already exist.

- "Findings" are not actionable until they are transformed into statements about how to do things in particular contexts. For example, "People are emotionally sensitive to color" is a finding, while "Change color palate to reflect changes in emotional tone" is an actionable design suggestion. "People like new challenges" translates into design rules like "Provide multiple levels of complexity in game-play," or "Build in a progression of play patterns."

- This one was particularly challenging for us as we designed storylines for Rockett's world. We had to work hard to avoid creating games where the "right" choices would always reflect how we wanted girls and women to behave. We wanted generosity and kindness and positive thinking to prevail. But sometimes, whining works. And regardless of how enlightened we may be, exclusion often has the desired result of bringing people back into line. The trick was to make our stories true to our research experience without abandoning our ideals.

Research as practice involves understanding people in different ways. Work based on a clear view of people—their lives, needs, and desires—will have the greatest likelihood of success. A project may start because there is a good business opportunity, or because an eccentric billionaire has a pet idea, or because you're on a mission from the goddess. Regardless of how it comes into being, a project's success has most to do with how values are applied. Different values come to the fore depending upon the task at hand.

When you are looking at popular culture, you will undoubtedly find patterns in the data that match something in yourself or the people you know and love. At this moment, you must make a crucial decision.

To be an honest researcher,
YOU MUST RESIST THE ENORMOUS TEMPTATION TO INTERPRET AS YOU GO

IN TERMS OF YOUR OWN EXPERIENCE AND VALUES.

Research ethics require that you approach your subject with an open mind and a question that does not contain its own answer. And it's a good idea to make the questions as general as is reasonable in order to have results that are broadly applicable. Be tough with your research plan. Clean up the places where your questions or methods are predisposing people to favor your idea. Ferret out all but the most fundamental assumptions you've made about your subjects. Blow up the barriers to bad news.

Once you have gathered, summarized, and analyzed your data, the next step is to turn those observations into design principles that are honed to a particular purpose. Now you have another really important decision to make: what are you going to do with what you know? Once you understand your potential customers, for example, how are you going to use that knowledge— to cater to their insecurities and cravings, or to find ways to make their lives more satisfying and productive? To exploit them or to love them?

Of course, the right answer is, to quote Captain James T. Kirk, "that third alternative"—namely, to make things that are relevant and enjoyable to people at the same time as you are doing things that lift them up and improve their lives over the long haul. You are going to use what you know about them to give people something that nourishes them. This is where you can reclaim the values you checked at the door.

Purple Moon might have chosen, as fashion and cosmetic companies often do, to take advantage of girls' insecurities in our product designs and marketing approach, and that approach might have turned out to be more lucrative. *A product that preys on personal weakness or perpetuates negative values may succeed, just as a product that expresses socially positive values may fail.* Purple Moon might just as well have failed following the Barbie model, but ignobly and without honor.

Because we came into the work with the intent of doing good for girls, we decided to use what we had learned about girls' social concerns, identity formation, and character preferences to offer material that would help them to discover the range of choices they could exercise in their own lives. Our games let girls play around with making different choices than they might make in the real world. They provided emotional rehearsal space for dealing with personally relevant issues and ethical dilemmas. When we combined our research findings with our values, we were able to produce design principles to guide us in our creative work that retained the integrity of both.

Humanistic values alone do not a business make. Once you have a strong product concept, business values must come to the front. To do good work in the context of popular culture requires you to build a healthy company that can succeed and endure. *Utopian entrepreneurs must understand the fundamentals of business practice, organization, and economics.*

It is always a balancing act, but positive social values will not save you in the absence of healthy investment partners and good business practices.

After years of avoiding Barbie-bashings in the name of good public relations, it feels so good to admit it publicly.

My daughters, each of whom had a passing childhood relationship with Barbie, know that I hate her. Although I did not forbid Barbie play, I felt no guilt about seizing teachable moments to preach about body and self-image. When Hilary was about five, she was carrying a Barbie doll through the kitchen of a feminist friend. "How can you let your child play with her?" my friend exclaimed in a tone of righteous indignation. "Hilary," I said, winding up for a good demo. "Tell Mona about anorexia."

"An-o-rex-i-a," Hilary recited. "That's when you think you are fat even though you aren't and so you die of skinny."

She held out Barbie in a supine position.

"It happened to one of Mommy's friends."

Over time, the girls came to cater to my special feelings about Barbie. One Halloween we decided to make Barbie into a crone, painting white-out on her hair and dressing her in a dark, ragged costume. A wad of masking tape produced a great dowager's hump. We experimented with lowering her bust line by holding a match under the indicated area, but this produced only melting, not sagging.

For my forty-fifth birthday, the girls created a special Barbie ceremony for me. "You might want to videotape this," Hilary advised. The two of them, dressed as executioners, brought a hapless Barbie into the kitchen and gravely placed her in the trash compactor. "Go ahead, Mom," Brooke offered. I turned the knob. After much loud grinding, we opened the compactor to find that

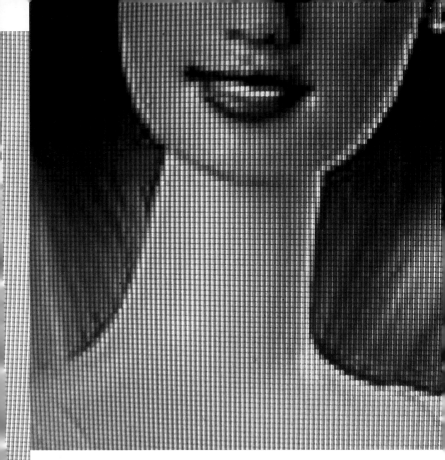

Barbie had survived completely intact. You have to hand it to Mattel for engineering a toy so durable.

I know all the reasons why Barbie is a supposed to be a great toy. I've had to list them many times with great equanimity in public talks. When girls move from babydolls to Barbie dolls, they are supposedly crossing into an area of fantasies about their own future identities. Barbie represents possibilities to girls— Fashion Model Barbie, Teacher Barbie, NBA Barbie, Dentist Barbie, Working Woman Barbie. She can be whatever a girl wants to pretend she is—a plastic-limbed scaffolding for imaginative play.

Nevertheless, I hate her.

i hate barbie

For me, Barbie was never about what was possible.
Au contraire, she was precisely about what was *im*possible.
Barbie was about who I could never be.
Blonde, fashionable, thin, confident. Not in a million years.

I think it may have been even harder than it is today to come by self-confidence as a little girl in the 50s. Feminism was certainly not a household word. Becoming a woman was presented as a process of perpetual self-editing, pruning yourself through will and discipline toward an ideal.

As a teen, I most often thought of myself as one of those miserable chimps dressed in frilly clothes at the circus. I was never popular; being smart, female, and nerdly was social suicide. Sometimes I wonder how different my life might have been if I had received the message that I was fine just as I was; that growing up wasn't about abandoning yourself to become an ideal woman, but about allowing the woman inside you to evolve. In my memory, Barbie is the earliest clear example of the unattainable.

I can forgive Ruth Handler, who invented Barbie in the 50s, and I can forgive Mattel, and I might even be able to forgive Jill Barad, who was my nemesis at Mattel when she was their CEO, but I can never forgive Barbie for how she made me feel.

"Well," Psychologist Barbie says,
"no one can make you feel anything.
You do that yourself.
It's not about me, it's about you."

As Eeyore would say, " thanks for noticin' me."

users, partners and fans. All of this research as
practice has to be directed toward something, of course, and of late that
something has been deemed "user experience." User experience is the buzz-
phrase fast becoming the new term for what was recently called "usability"
or "interface design" or "human-computer interaction." Before that it was
called "human factors," drawn from the aerospace industry and the study
of human pilots, or "man-machine interaction," used in connection with
guys in white coats standing in front of giant mainframes. If you don't
know what those guys look like, you can still see one: he's the icon for
Norton Utilities.

User experience as a label is a step in the right direction because it
puts the emphasis on something broader than what we used to call the
interface—the controls or the contact surface of a program. The term user
experience attempts to put us in touch with the entire experience that a
person has in a computer-based activity. I think what still doesn't work,
though, is that demeaning little word, "user." This term implies an unbal-
anced power relationship—the experts make things; everybody else is just
a user. People don't like to think of themselves as users. We like to see ourselves as creative, energetic beings who put out as much as we take in.

To see how this matters, try plugging in other words.

Customer—this person is highly valued and is usually right.

Audience—this person likes to watch and expects to be entertained.

Client—this person wants professional services.

Player—this person wants to have fun.

Participant—well, this person is doing something, whether it's fun or not.

Partner—this person has agreed to work on something together
with you.

The idea of being in partnership with the people purchasing your products or on your site is not only emotionally attractive; it is quite literally true. As my good friend (and CEO of Cheskin Research) Christopher Ireland taught me, products people really love are products that make people feel good about themselves. In this way, brand identity is very closely related to personal identity.

Purple-Moon.com really tried to meld brand identity with personal identity, and in some ways we succeeded beyond our wildest expectations. Our story offers some good examples of how to create and sustain a community. For the success of a brand or a set of characters, an active fan culture may not be sufficient, but it sure is necessary. Our understanding of how fan cultures work was greatly informed by the work of Henry Jenkins, founder of the Comparative Media Studies Program at M.I.T. With his help, we identified some key ingredients in the fan-culture starter kit. First and foremost, fans need to be able to "appropriate cultural material to construct personal meaning." This is culture-theory-speak for being able to fool around with characters and their universe and create your own stuff with them. *Star Trek* slash video, fiction, and 'zines are probably the best examples of this kind of activity. Paramount Studios—*Star Trek's* "owners" —has been clever enough to coopt some of that fan energy and turn it into profit through official novels and fanzines. The fact that *Trek* fan culture survives despite Paramount's vigorous prosecution of "poachers" is due to the extraordinary level of brand loyalty, and also to the tenacity and cunning of *Star Trek* fans, who will **stop at nothing** short of anonymous servers in the outer solar system to strut their stuff. In general, however, the reflexive desire of businesses to protect their "intellectual property" by stomping on unauthorized use of characters and narrative worlds is actually a pretty bad idea, because it serves to discourage the central activity of fandom.

You can encourage and nurture a fan community by providing ways for fans to create and publish their own content based on your world. The ability to create your own version of the first-person shooter game *Doom* is a great example. Another is George Lucas' brilliant move to allow publication of fan-created movies with his *Star Wars* materials. Purple Moon published *Rockett's Adventure Maker* to let kids create new characters in the Rockett art style and then put them into our world and combine them with our characters in a comic strip format. On the Web, we published questionnaires and used the results in the design of new CD-ROM products. We ran writing contests based on story starters and published the winners on the site; we published girls' submissions to the Whistling Pines newspaper and girl-authored poetry and prose; and we helped girls to create and publish their own personal pages. We were surprised and delighted to discover that girls were using the postcard system on the site to arrange swap meets for Purple Moon treasures. *They formed clubs within the site based on treasures, zodiac signs, sports interests, animals, geographic location, and favorite characters. They also spun off independent fan sites.*

One of the limits to Purple Moon's growth as a small, independent company was the difficulty of getting our characters exposure beyond interactive media. That big TV deal never quite closed. Fan behavior kicks in only when characters are sufficiently familiar and deemed to be personally relevant. Purple Moon's fandom was small in comparison with the mass media products I've mentioned here, but it was large and extremely active compared to other interactive properties with similar reach. I think we can attribute that to two factors: the affordances offered by the Website, and the appeal of the characters and their world.

Donald Norman introduced the idea of affordances in his early work on user-centered design. An affordance is a kind of (real or metaphorical) handle—a feature of a thing that suggests and facilitates a kind of action one might take.
Creating the affordances for people to construct their own identities and communities is key successful culture work. Supporting personalization is a powerful and graceful way to acknowledge and celebrate difference. In a networked world, allowing detailed self-representation will assist tremendously in the formation of online communities.

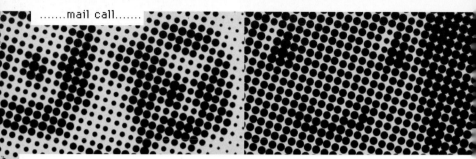

When we first launched the Purple-Moon.com site, we let kids send postcards to characters and we responded to them in the characters' voices. I personally thought that this would be a very cool way to employ moms in chenille bathrobes stuck at home with a bunch of kids—helping the Web fulfill the promise of providing actual employment—but I was advised that this plan would be too difficult to recruit and administer. So folks in the studio started answering the postcards, which were rapidly becoming an avalanche. People chose the characters they felt most resonant with. Our female Story Director answered rocker boy Ruben Rosale's email; the male receptionist donned a rhinestone bracelet and plunged enthusiastically into channeling fashion-queen character Nicole.

Thousands of heartfelt, personal postcards poured in for the characters—asking for advice, giving advice, befriending some characters and chastising others for being mean. With six or seven folks working on it full time, we were falling farther behind every day. After several weeks we were so swamped that we had to ask girls to back off. The principal of our fictitious Whistling Pines Junior High, Mrs. Herrera, explained to our girls that the characters weren't getting their school work done because they were spending too much time on email and asked everybody to help by sending fewer post cards. Eventually we moved to a bulletin-board style of communication because we didn't have the budget to respond personally to each postcard, but the numbers of girls who visited and registered continued to grow.

Although I have never been a serious gamer, I have always loved game designers. The audacious nerdliness, the technical wizardry, even the generally poor hygiene was exotically attractive to me. One of the reasons I cofounded the Computer Game Developers' Conference in 1989 was to be near these people and to hear them talk.

The second year of the conference, I nominated Dan Bunten to give the after-dinner keynote. I genuinely admired Dan's work. His football game didn't interest me, although I was often told it was the best in the business, but I was a great fan of *Seven Cities of Gold* and *M.U.L.E.*, the first truly cooperative videogame. The fact that he created these games inside the belly of the boy-game beast—Electronic Arts—made him a hero to me. He was tall, red-haired, soft-spoken, with a luscious Arkansas drawl that made me want to curl up and purr. I finally got to spend some time with Dan after his talk in 1990. Although he was an outrageous flirt, underneath the surface was a shy and thoughtful person with a wonderful sense of humor.

By 1993 the Computer Game Developers' Conference had quadrupled in attendance and had moved upscale to the Sheraton in San Jose. The dinner event was always a masquerade, and that year I had decided to show up as my fictitious brother, Chuck. **Chuck is a Vietnam veteran, longtime hippie** denizen of Humboldt County, where he pursues illicit agriculture and computer game design.

Under his own label of AlterEgo, Chuck had been working on a game involving fractals for about seven years. The story we put out was that Chuck came to the CGDC to fill in for me as an award presenter during the dinner, as I had family emergency. I was really looking forward to introducing Chuck to Dan Bunten.

It took me about three hours to make Chuck's beard, hair by hair with spirit gum, as I had learned in acting school. Chuck wore tattered jeans and sported a stringy brown ponytail. My friend (now husband) Rob Tow helped me invent Chuck and hold up his identity at the conference. Rob took a Polaroid photo and made him a laminated AlterEgo badge, which he wore clipped to his army jacket. Rob and I were shocked to discover that Chuck is one ugly guy. He is even shorter than I am, and his bone structure is all wrong.

Chuck does not know how to behave appropriately in public. During the pre-dinner reception, he got into a loud argument about the redwoods in Humboldt with an old friend of mine who did not recognize me at a distance of sixteen inches. Chuck flirted crassly with the few women in attendance. By the time he walked into the banquet room, he was alarmingly obnoxious. He swaggered impatiently from table to table, looking for Dan. What he found brought him to a full stop.

Dan was in drag, too—impressively realistic drag. His hair was shoulder-length and redder than usual; his clothing came from the pages of Ladies' Home Journal. He was wearing glasses with big, pinkish frames. His nails were done. He wasn't kidding. Dan had had a sex change, and Danielle was coming out among friends—the thousand or so game designers who had always been her community.

She rose to embrace Chuck, a full foot taller than he in her heels. She was gracious. I felt increasingly idiotic as her sincerity and bravery sank in. Chuck fumbled through the rest of the program, retired to his room early, and never attended the conference again. Back in my own persona, I had a nightcap with Danielle. I asked her how the community was handling her transformation. Judging from the adolescent, sometimes sneering portrayal of females in the games of the time, one might have expected some ridicule and sniggering. Instead, she was being treated with a kind of gentle protectiveness. In their support for Danielle, I saw yet another reason why I love game designers. The next day, I made Danielle a present of one of my most precious possessions, my grandmother's favorite rhinestone earrings. I wanted to welcome her to the sisterhood.

A few months later, as I was struggling with the germ of the idea of emotional navigation as an interface to a computer game for girls, it occurred to me to call Danielle and ask her to collaborate with me. She was the most accomplished and innovative game designer I knew. David Liddle agreed that I needed "a playmate my own age" and Dani was hired as a consultant.

She swept into Interval in a crisp white shirt and jeans, curly red hair flying, excited as a little kid at a party. Over the six months that we worked together, Dani and I became close friends—girlfriends. We talked about feminism, fashion, psychotherapy, empathy, and self-esteem. Dan had been a friend of mine, too, but to both of us, he was another person from another time.

mad so far, I told her about my idea for emotional navigation—that is, **getting around in a game on the basis of how the character is feeling.**

We hit upon the shorthand of "mad-sad-glad." Dani was inspired by Lucille Ball to cook up a game concept called "Dinner Is Ruined" with which we could try out the interface. The idea was based on playing house, where emotions led to different outcomes in the kitchen. Fooling around with her Hypercard prototype, we realized that playing house was too young for our target audience. I came up with the alternative of being the new kid in school. The new kid could focus on peer relationships, which are center stage for preteen girls. Dani went home to Little Rock to work with the concept.

When she returned a few weeks later, she said she needed to have a serious talk with me. We went out into the courtyard at Interval. She lit a cigarette and started to cry. **"I can't do this, Brenda," she said. "I just don't have the right experiences.**

I didn't grow up a girl."

Despite all my arguments, she was determined to resign. Although she assured me that the concept was great, she believed that she had taken the project as far as she could. I would have to find new collaborators to go the rest of the distance.

We kept in touch over the next few years and got together whenever she was in town. She went on to do more wonderful inventing for M-Path, one of the first companies to address the idea of multiplayer gaming over the internet. She came to the wedding when Rob and I were married in 1994. Hilary was seriously pissed when Dani caught the bouquet. "It's not fair!" Hilary whined. "She's six feet tall!"

In 1997 Danielle was diagnosed with lung cancer. She died in early 1998. I dedicated Purple Moon's first two games to her. She was a great lady.

storytelling and values. The relationship between

culture and identity is a crucial leverage point for making real change in people's lives. We construct ourselves out of two deeply intermingled kinds of material: our life experiences, and our cultural context. In other words, who we are is the product of both the stories we hear and the stories of our lives. This dynamic is at work in the identities of children and adults, girls and boys, men and women.

Storytelling is a nurturing art. It is not simply the transmission of narrative material. It is a purposeful action that is intended to communicate, to teach, to heal.

STORIES ARE CONTENT;

STORYTELLING IS RELATIONSHIP.

Throughout our history, cultures, families, and individual lives have been held together by Webs of storytelling relationships.

We are all familiar with the sort of grand storytelling that happens at the level of a culture at large. The Homeric myths, classical Greek drama, the plays of Shakespeare are of such a scale. The traditions of bardic storytelling and theatre, and more recently the forms of fiction and film, have continuously provided the means for grand storytelling.

Such stories enable a culture to behold itself as a whole.

They function as illuminations that help us to

see where we are, how we have gotten here, what is important,

and where we should go.

But grand storytelling fills only part of our species'

need for narrative.

What stories will shape our future? Written in the 1990s, Kim Stanley Robinson's trilogy of *Red Mars*, *Green Mars*, **and** *Blue Mars* **is award-winning, best-selling science fiction. But it is more than that. The Apollo program owed a significant debt of gratitude to H.G. Wells, Robert Heinlein, and Arthur C. Clarke. The NASA Mars team has been so inspired by the Mars Trilogy that they've adopted a flag based on Robinson's books—bars of** red, green, and blue. **Going to Mars is a very cool story—certainly more motivating than the story in which the space program devolves into a missile defense system or a bunch of private companies schlepping cargo around and launching communication satellites. Going to Mars is a story that would involve big government expenditures, even treaties. The tiny-minded, tax-cutting, strong-defense-and-screw-science flavor of politicians see no point in sending people to Mars. But lots of our young people do. And they'd be eager to learn a lot of math and physics and biology and chemistry in order to get there. The dream of going to Mars is coming up for our kids. As my eldest daughter says, "** Your generation had Woodstock and the moon landing. We get immortality and Mars. **" Remember how the space program focused and motivated young people thirty years ago? To see that kind of excitement in a kid's eyes again would be worth the cost of the program, even without the obvious benefits it offers to science, technology, and the future of space travel.**

There are many other kinds of stories floating around in our culture—comics, novels, urban legends, tabloid tales of lottery winners and celebrity affairs. Contemporary media—especially television—allow us to feel as if we are always in touch, always looking through our electronic window at the living heart of our culture, quintessential residents of Marshall McLuhan's global village.

Through common media, we have the illusion of relationship. But a talk-show host is not your grandmother, or your sister, or a friend who knows and cares about you. We are vitally interested in the news even though, as Neil Postman has observed, the news generally consists of stories that happened somewhere else to other people and about which we can take no meaningful action. Grand storytelling functions fairly well in mass media, but personal storytelling—the giving of a tale by an individual as a teaching or healing for a particular group or person—is an endangered human sensibility.

The art of personal storytelling is still alive in some ethnic and regional cultures, and the practice of live storytelling as concert-style entertainment has gained popularity in recent years. But there is evidence of a continuing decline in the practice of parents telling or reading stories to their children. Personal family storytelling is increasingly replaced by television, video and audio tapes, and other mass media. For most American children, storytelling exists, if at all, as a novelty encountered in a school assembly. Luckily, interventions are afoot. Culture workers such as the late Dana Atchley, Joe Lambert and Nina Mullen, Abbe Don, and Nathan Shedroff have created environments, tools, and examples that inspire an ever-growing digital storytelling community. Every day, more people discover the power of the Web as a storytelling medium. "Weblogs" are a kind of personal meta-storytelling that has been enabled entirely by the Web. As online storytelling pioneer Derek Powazek observes, "Sure, they're full of links. They're

also full of lives."

As part of our research for Purple Moon, we tested a variety of story-related concepts, including both personal storytelling and folktales, that we later incorporated into the structure of the *Secret Paths* series of games. We were surprised that stories raised a red flag with some parents. I remember one concerned father in Los Angeles saying, "This product seems to be a lot about values. But whose values are these? Why should I trust them? I'm not sure I want a computer teaching values to my daughter." A bit later in the session we asked that same father how he felt about the values represented in games like **Mortal Combat** and **Killer Instinct**. Unhesitatingly, he replied, " Oh, those games don't have any values in them.

They're not about values."

What a stunning revelation! The values embedded in mainstream videogames are so pervasive and so unquestioned that they were virtually invisible to this concerned parent. But of course, when a child is engaged in story play—with or without a computer—the whole person is involved in imaginative construction. The values category is hanging wide open, soaking things up, trying things out, and if we do not design what goes into it, we are nevertheless responsible for what falls in there by default. Stories function like cultural DNA, passing values down through the generations.

Stories, movies, videogames, and Websites don't have to be about values to have a profound influence on values.
Values are everywhere,
embedded in every aspect of our culture and lurking in the very natures of our media and our technologies. Culture workers know the question isn't whether they are there but who is taking responsibility for them, how they are being shaped, and how they are shaping us and our future.

Whatever else may be true of 21C, we can assume that the changes it brings will be profound and the rate of change will accelerate.
I was born in 1950 and I've seen a whole lot of change. When I was a kid, for example, there were fewer than half as many people in the world as there are today.

It really was like Pleasantville. My grandpa worked for the railroad and my grandma did a lot of sewing and managed a grocery store. My dad was a city planner—a civil servant—and my mom kept house and worked in sales promotion for an insurance company. They paid cash for most everything and kept their money in a savings account. They worked hard at being in the middle class and they were content to be there. In my lily-white high school, I learned that there was a correct answer for every question. I still have nightmares in which I have to go back to Indiana and give all those right answers. The illusion that change consisted only of benign forms of progress was shattered for me in the great cultural discontinuity of the late 60s. For this, I am grateful.

Many of the rules and stories that I grew up with—even venerable stuff like proverbs and Greek myths—don't seem entirely applicable in today's world. One of the stories that doesn't work very well these days is Aesop's fable, "The Tortoise and the Hare." As you will recall, in the original story, the Tortoise wins the race because the Hare is an over-confident slacker. Here's how the story might go today:

One day a hare was boasting of his running speed and laughing at the tortoise for being so slow. Much to the hare's surprise the tortoise challenged him to a race. The hare, looking on the whole affair as a great joke, readily consented. The race began and the hare, of course, soon left the tortoise far behind and went on to beat him handily. It was probably the case that the tortoise thought the hare would stop and fool around and maybe take a nap. But the tortoise failed to notice that the hare did everything fast and hard. He drove fast and he talked fast and he ate fast and he ran fast. He traded hot stocks on his handheld during boring business meetings. No time was wasted. The tortoise, on the other hand, felt that his maturity and balance made him superior to the hare, and if he worked steadily and paid his bills on time, he would do well in the end. The hare made millions on internet stocks before the NASDAQ crashed, and his fortunes sent several generations of little hares to the best colleges. After retirement, the tortoise was unable to survive in the city on his shrinking social security checks, so he ended up living in the park.

Okay, what's wrong with that story? It's cynical. It doesn't give good advice about how to live. We probably don't want our children to believe it, even though some of us may be afraid that it's true. One of our perennial fears about technology is that as technology gets better at telling stories (through means like virtual reality and special effects), people—especially kids— will be increasingly unable to distinguish reality from illusion. But to my mind, the danger isn't technology; it's the stories of our times that pose the greatest threat to our children and our future. Stories are tools for knowing and judging.

Change the stories, and you change how people live.

In our part of the world, the lead story has been about money for so long that we treat distinct domains of human endeavor—work, value, science, education, politics—as though they collapsed into a single category. Due no doubt to a steady diet of advertising, as well as the sustained prosperity Americans have enjoyed for most of the last two decades, money is the language of our culture.

The story I learned about work when I was growing up was that the idea was to create value. The goal was to make things that would make people's lives better. If you could create something of value, then you could hope for—even expect—to be rewarded with some money. If you did your job well, you would also reap spiritual rewards—not the least of which was happiness. In this story you can recognize the Aristotelian idea of virtue. The old Greek guy said that happiness is virtue, and virtue consists in fulfilling a worthy function well. In today's business climate, the story is not about producing value, but about

PRODUCING MONEY.

And the "happiness as virtue" part has gone missing altogether. In the "new economy," quality, service, and value in the old-fashioned sense are not typically part of the conversation. The dot-com story was: get there first, build it fast, cash out. Facing fears of downturn, we seem willing to accept the degradation of public education, environmental protection, social services, and public health in order to keep business booming and consumers' money flowing.

The story of money has conflated two other categories that, although related, are appropriately distinct: economic prosperity and public good.

ALL BOATS DO NOT NECESSARILY RISE WHEN MORE PEOPLE ARE RICH — WITNESS THE GROWING HOMELESS POPULATIONS OF OUR CITIES.

All boats do not necessarily rise when people pay lower taxes. Institutions such as public education and public transportation were designed to express our collective commitment to the public good. When public funding for such programs is eliminated, what do we do instead? Support them through charity? Altruism can do many things, but charity probably can't build and run a public transit system.

In the story where prosperity equals public good, free enterprise should run the public transit system—and they would do it more efficiently than government. But they'd probably have to run it at a loss, and would therefore not be allowed by their shareholders to run it for long, because the unquantifiable benefits—the prevention of pollution and the ability for low-income workers to get to their jobs—cannot be shown as revenue on the balance sheet. It's similarly hard to make a business plan for public education.

When is the right solution government, and when is it private enterprise, and when is it charity? It's enough to make a voter's brain hurt. But in the story where prosperity magically takes care of the public good,

all I have to do to take care of America is make more MONEY AND SPEND IT.

You see, this story is easier to understand and easier to live. And that is why it is dangerous.

Many of the shapers of our democracy—Washington, Jefferson, Hamilton, Madison—began their political lives at tender ages. They read the classics in Greek and Latin and studied the stories of Athens, Rome, and the republic of Venice. They were well-educated kids looking for action— more precisely, for the ability to take action in the arena of government and politics. For young people today, the desire to take action is much more likely to eventuate in a purchase than a vote. We've taught them how to be good consumers, you see, but not necessarily how to be good citizens, for informed citizens are inherently more dangerous to the powers that be than are desirous consumers.

Our kids—and our democracy—are going to be in pretty bad shape if education and political participation continue to decline. We hope that our teens will blossom into an informed populace, a generation that can produce great leaders and good governance. To quote Thomas Jefferson, "Whenever people are well-informed they can be trusted with their own government." The corollary is, when people aren't well-informed, they're likely to wake up one morning to find that their government—and their lives—don't belong to them any more.

One way to look at these issues is to consider them in terms of agency. Being able to see the effects of our actions is what gives us the sense of agency or personal power—a feeling that young people are particularly hungry for. I can see the result of a purchase; it is harder to see the result of a vote. I can see the result of having more money; it is harder to see the result of funding for public education. The effects of our tax dollars are hard to see unless we know where and how to look. And most often they fall in the nondramatic category—take the essentially boring story of Y2K, a massive technological breakdown that would have been a lot more exciting than the fact that it was prevented. The news doesn't talk about the fact that your taxes are the bridge that didn't collapse, the kid who didn't rob the 7-11, the person who didn't freeze to death in a doorway. Hard to see, hard to sell, so to speak.

Unless, perhaps, you are able to visualize the web of causes and effects, to look for patterns and explore alternatives, to see how different choices and actions can have different outcomes. One of the most highly leveraged actions we can take with our burgeoning technological power is to improve our ability to make interactive simulations of complex systems. Simulations that help us visualize causality and evaluate options can help us make better judgments about many kinds of things. They can help us make both business and government more efficient and more accountable. They can influence what young people see as valuable in education, how we help them learn, and what they decide to do with their lives.

If Moore's law continues to operate—and there's no reason to think it won't—steadily increasing computing power will make interactive simulations easier to create, and decreasing costs will make them easier to distribute. In ten years, the equivalent of today's most powerful chip will probably cost about 50 cents—and that's a conservative estimate. You'll be able to paper the walls with them.

Creating interactive simulations of complex systems is one of the most highly leveraged goals we can achieve with our burgeoning technological power.

Why? Because the ability to visualize complex webs of causality and to evaluate alternative courses of action will become increasingly vital as the century proceeds.

Interactive simulations are not a new idea. People have been working on them for several decades, but the art is far from perfected. We still can't make simulations that accurately predict the weather or the stock market. But as we improve our interactive simulations of complex systems, we open up new spaces for thinking about the issues, discovering connections and alternatives, and creating and testing models of system dynamics. Our ability to create robust simulations improves literally every day, and working with them makes us better thinkers.

Good simulations will not only help us learn about systems, they may help us evaluate policies and form political goals. Simulations can also strengthen accountability by helping us to understand the effects of actions taken by particular companies, industries, or governments. For example, it is already possible to obtain information about the specific types and sources of pollution in a particular environment. Using such data as the basis for an interactive simulation will make a more convincing case for accountability. It will also allow both citizens and companies to explore the consequences of changes in industrial practices. With work, we may be able to simulate some of the social dimensions of the problem as well.

Robust economic and social simulations are an important frontier. A central challenge in simulation is the diversity of data types involved—geological and geographical data are less diverse and therefore more tractable than biological data; economic data is less diverse than social and behavioral data, and so on.

Another challenge is designing visual and sensory interfaces to simulations so that they are accessible to both professionals and citizens. These challenges are technically achievable and should be seen as important research targets in both private and public sectors. Utopian entrepreneurs can devise uses for simulation that can be made into viable businesses in the near term. For example, the fields of molecular biology, agriculture, energy conservation, and the management of water and other natural resources offer significant entrepreneurial opportunities.

In these few years the internet has been with us, we've all become aware of its enormous potential to make us larger than our individual selves. **Our collective intelligence is enhanced by distributed memory and distributed expertise.**

We can also add distributed computing to the toolbox, as exemplified by the devoted community of people who volunteer cycles from their PCs to help meet the massive computational needs of the Search for Extraterrestrial Intelligence (SETI). The idea of citizen participation in distributed computing for very large projects is now being extended into areas such as weather modeling and genomics. As computing power continues to grow and prices to drop, people have the capacity to engage in projects larger than their own desktops for scientific, altruistic, or imaginative reasons. This activity is new in the world, and offers new resources to the utopian entrepreneur concerned about developing relationships more with those who define themselves as citizens than with those who define themselves as consumers.

Just as simulation technology will provide better means for representing the possible effects of our choices in the real world, it may also enable us finally to create satisfying **interactive fiction**.

The interactive story is a hypothetical beast in the mythology of computing, an elusive unicorn we can imagine but have yet to capture.

We can glimpse the possibilities in work like Will Wright's *Sims* and Joe Bates' *Woggles*. But even if interactive stories are technically possible, no one has yet produced a canonical example.

Like other literary and artistic forms, interactive fiction will emerge through experimentation and successive approximations. According to reader response theory and other theories of projective construction in narrative, linear stories we might read or hear are already highly interactive in that the meaning of the story is constructed by the reader in collaboration with the author.

In the Purple Moon Rockett series, we explored interactive uses for what writers call

"back story"

—the facts and feelings that lie beneath the surface narrative. *We arrived at the idea of placing back-story elements such as journals, notes, and artifacts in characters' lockers. Locker contents could change depending upon player's choices and the passage of time.* Our writers and artists also created back-story elements that could be found on the Whistling Pines Website, in the school newspaper, and in the yearbook office. Players and fans were encouraged to create new back-story materials through activities on the Website and in the context of individual games. Both kinds of affordances drew on the power of narrative construction as a play pattern.

The click-and-reveal interaction in the original *Living Books* games
embodied a more open-ended approach to the same
play pattern.

Hypertexts

and branching structures represent another approach to interactive
fiction. "Choose your own adventure" books use these techniques. Of
course, computers offer us vastly more space than printed books for creating range and subtlety in branching narratives. Purple Moon's Rockett
series represented branching alternatives as mood choices for characters
as they encountered various situations. Although generations of games
prove they can work well when they are well crafted, branching architec-
tures have two inherent limitations. One is the combinatorial explosion
that can result if the branching tree is not pruned. The other is the fact that
each branch must be authored—an extremely labor-intensive endeavor.

Virtual reality

offers another view of interactive fiction, if one sees that a narrative
can be retrospectively constructed about a person's experience in a
virtual world. In the late 80s, a limiting factor of VR's potential was that no
one could imagine uses beyond military and industrial training simulations. I thought that making an imaginative counter-example could set VR
free of that constraint. The result was a work called *Placeholder*, which,
although it was experienced by fewer than two hundred people,
pointed to new uses
for VR.

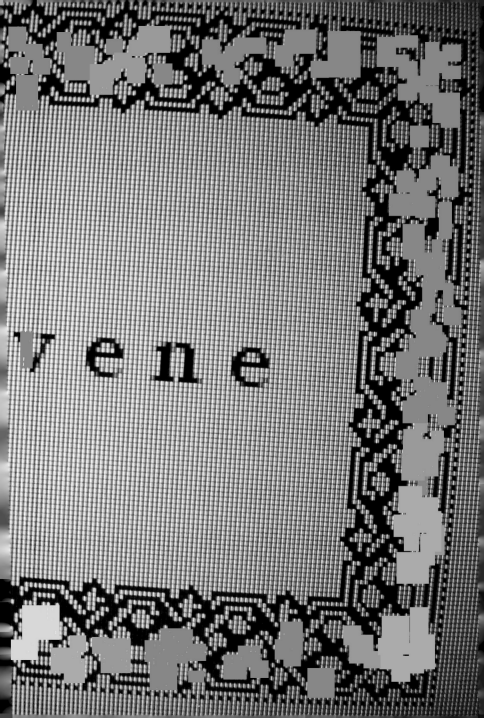

In 1993, artist and videographer Rachel Strickland and I received a grant from Canada's Banff Centre to produce a virtual reality project based on the local landscape. Interval Research provided additional funding. Our goal was to explore relationships between landscape, stories, and play. My daughters, then ages 5 and 7, came with me, and every morning we woke up to the gorgeous sight of Mount Rundle. One day the girls told me that they had invented something new. They had taped cardboard knobs onto the sill under the picture window. "Look, Mom, it's Mountain TV—all mountain, all the time! And listen to this, the weather and light you see on this TV is exactly the same as it is outside! Only one channel, but it's a great picture!" In many ways the best part of the project was location scouting. We hiked to waterfalls, caves, mountain overlooks, glaciers, and lakes.

With colleagues Michael Naimark, Rob Tow, John Harrison, and many other folks from the Banff Centre and Interval, we created three connected virtual environments, each of which was a representation of an actual place in the local Canadian land-scape. The cave was a dark, drippy space, represented primarily as a 3-D acoustic environment that revealed its shapes and textures through sound. We represented a stand of hoodoos as a tiled globe of photographic images, and a high waterfall in the forest as a full-motion video relief projection. With actors from the Precipice Theatre Company, we used improvisation in the landscape as a technique for developing characters drawn from folktales and rock art.

You could enter the *Placeholder* world in the company of another person, each stepping into a magic circle and donning a head-mounted display and two simple hand sensors. The journey would begin—for obvious Jungian reasons—in the cave. At first, you could see the other participant only as the tiny points of light that defined her hands (not just the right one, by the way, as was customary in the days of the DataGlove).

Presently, you would notice large, luminous petroglyphs of animals on the cave walls—Snake, Fish, Spider, and Crow. When you approached them, the animals began to speak about themselves and to beckon you to "come closer." So, for example, Crow might say, "I am the eye of the world. I see all that shines and glitters." If you came all the way up to him and your head intersected with the petroglyph, you would become embodied as Crow—that is, the other participant would suddenly see the Crow body change color and begin to move around. If you spoke, your voice would now sound like Crow's voice, and—this is the best part—if you flapped your arms, you found that you could fly. Each animal had distinct sensory-motor characteristics. We called these animal suits "smart costumes." Spiral-shaped petroglyphs acted as portals between the worlds. In all the worlds, you could leave voicemarks—audio graffiti—in special virtual rocks called voiceholders. People left messages and stories, and constructed story lattices by arranging the voiceholders in different ways. I think of *Placeholder* as an intervention because

we created it with the conscious intention of being able to tell a different story

about virtual reality in hopes of influencing the future of the medium. For example, at that time, most people were still describing VR as out-of-body experiences in artificial worlds. The point of asking humans beings to "put on" the bodies of animals was to bring people's attention to the fact that they have bodies in VR, more than the traditional floating virtual hand. The point of modeling natural environments was to address the common fear that VR would "replace the real world" for people who became addicted to it. Our intent was to invert this idea—to use VR, as Ansel Adams used photography, to point to beauty; to say, "notice this;" to honor and celebrate the natural world and the ways it articulates with our imaginations.

Following *Placeholder*, Char Davies' exquisite works *Osmose* (1996) and *Ephemère* (1998) further expanded the vision of what VR could accomplish in aesthetic and spiritual dimensions. These interventions may have freed VR from being pigeonholed exclusively as a training tool, but they did not rescue it from banality. With today's desktop VR solutions,

the experience too often consists of
wandering around in
a forest of weird polygons
dressed in an avatar body,
HAVING TEXTUAL CONVERSATIONS
WITH OTHER FUNNY-LOOKING
AVATARS

that are about as uplifting as the dialogue in chat rooms. Big VR producers like Silicon Graphics have abandoned head-mounted displays for instrumented command chairs and wraparound screens, impoverishing the kinesthetic dimension of the experience. Likewise, most university centers for VR development have abandoned real, walk- or fly-around VR for the command-chair approach. Hopefully, we will see advances in head-mounted display technology that give us back our bodies in VR.

Three forces are coming together that may enable us to resurrect the incredible imaginative potential of VR: increasing computer power, high-speed networking, and the rise of online multiplayer gaming. So far, utopian entrepreneurs with brilliant concepts for building simulation-based multiplayer worlds with VR-like interfaces have failed to secure funding. Like many pioneers, they are ahead of their time—multiplayer gaming is still in its infancy, and high-speed, high-bandwidth connections are not yet commonly available. And—oops!—there is not yet a good business model for this new kind of experience.

Cultural innovation

can only proceed hand in hand with

technological and economic innovation.

invention and inversion. Reality has always been too

small for human imagination, but we have a remarkable knack for augmenting it. I loved the VR boom of the late 80s and early 90s, and although the heat of that period has cooled, the technologies of presence still promise to open new worlds—real and imaginary—to the body and senses. Remote presence technologies allow us to take action in worlds that are real but remote from our own bodies, through either distance or scale. As the new century begins, VR and remote presence are being extended into new dimensions, from microsurgery to Mars.

One reason VR had such a cultural impact is that the technology brought about an inversion. It was not a logical successor to the brain-in-a-box. In fact, **VR turned computers inside out.** The brain-in-a-box computer has no body; VR uses our bodies as its instrument and gives us a first-person view. Computers—even today's frisky little laptops—immobilize the body in front of a keyboard and screen; conversely, VR relies upon human movement and kinesthetic sensations to achieve its effect. Ethnobotanist and philosopher Terence McKenna mused that this fascination with turning things inside out is what made us manifest VR in the first place—to create an instrumentality that could, as he put it, "textualize the world and exteriorize the soul." The inversion inherent in VR engaged the public's imagination,

and it became a cultural magnet for the

hopes,

fears,

and inventive

energies

of the time.

Turning things inside out is an extremely powerful technique. In fact, inversions have given us some of our greatest leaps in culture, technology, and consciousness. In his book, *Myths to Live By* (1972), Joseph Campbell describes the change in consciousness that resulted from our first view of the earth from space. *Seeing our blue planet alone in the starry blackness, Campbell says, we suddenly understood that rather than coming into this world, we come out of it,* or as Alan Watts put it, "as a vine grapes, so the Earth peoples." This inversion had a lot to do with the impact of the Gaia hypothesis, both as a new line of scientific thinking and a new popular mythology for our relationship to our planet.

More recently, the idea of a robot as a unitary, humanlike central intelligence with an artificial body has been brilliantly inverted by folks like Rodney Brooks at M.I.T., whose theory of subsumption architecture challenged both the traditional idea of robots and the reigning notion of artificial intelligence. Manuela Veloso designed souped-up Sony "AIBO" robot dogs to play soccer in teams. Similariy, a swarm of communication-enhanced robot "bugs" will replace the unitary lander on future Mars missions. This approach spreads the reach—and the risk—of robotic planetary exploration.

In 1983, aliens killed a two-billion-dollar company.
Superman had worked it over, but it was ET who landed
the final blow. **It was ugly.**
I was there, but I escaped the worst of
the carnage.
The remains were buried in concrete somewhere in New Mexico.
For those of you too young to remember,
the victim was a company called Atari. What killed it was a sort
of Dr. Frankenstein attempt at what we called repurposing.
The company was owned by Warner and run by a band of
executives from the world of consumer products. None of them
had a computer on his desk. They held the simple belief that
a great license would yield a great videogame.

The Atari corporation paid very little attention to
designing for computer games, a medium that is quite different
from films or comic books. And so no one except a few isolated
programmers who actually built the games was looking at the
requirements for good interactivity, play patterns, or design
principles. There was no market research on what players liked
in a game. When it was determined that a movie was a hit with
the target audience (yes, 14-year-old boys), a license to produce
a game based on the movie was acquired. The task was lobbed
at a programmer who was typically given about three months to
write the code.

At the same time, hordes of Harvard MBAs began churning out business plans, and transplants from aerospace middle management drew up elaborate production schedules, and Procter & Gamble veterans happily began planning marketing and distribution. Great commercials were produced. Except for the programmers, however, no one was in the business of creating great videogames.

And so, Atari published some really bad products, and lo, **the customers did rise up and smite them**. So began the great videogame darkness of 1984 that lasted until almost the end of that decade. A wiser industry emerged, but only a little wiser.

The Children's Television Workshop never came up to speed on producing computer games from its properties, and Disney arrived very late at success in the game business, given the strength of its properties and the breadth of its market. Carmen Sandiego, a computer game character, managed to get herself a TV series, and *Power Rangers* and *Teenage Mutant Ninja Turtles* and *X-Men* have had moderately successful transmedia lives as well. Even though comics make perhaps the best candidates for transmedia treatment, it's worth noting that it's still a stretch (as in yellow tights), and you can always spot the media type of the root property.

My point, and I do have one, is that the transmedia process has thus far consisted of repurposing content from one medium for another—film to TV, comics to film, dolls and toys to videogames, movies to dolls and toys, or movies to the Web. In a transmedia world, where you know from the start that you want to produce content that will appear across several media types and delivery devices, repurposing is an inelegant and inefficient solution. **We need to develop a new methodology.**

At the beginning of this book, I wrote about the four big new ideas in the world of computer technology with which I've had the good fortune to be involved—personal computers, computer games, virtual reality, and the Web. I see the same kind of energy building around *the idea of convergence today. But it doesn't seem to be happening quite the way we pictured it.* The forced, unnatural coupling of the Web and television, for example, has failed to achieve convergence because the distinctions in situated context are too large. We will see Web-enabled TV and video-enabled Web, but these two media are different and will continue to be so, even though related content will appear in both of them.

Convergence is occurring at a lower level, where all media types boil down to a packet-based

SOUP,

an IP sea in which all devices swim.

Using the trick of inversion, we get a different picture: a divergence of displays and devices address ever-finer distinctions in the situated contexts of their use. Pagers, radios, phones, movies, TV, email, games, Websites become formal containers that receive and transmit content from professional authors, fan communities, and regular folks.

What is emerging is what we might call

transmedia culture.

People have an enduring interest in content and a continuing propensity to be fans of content properties. But they will access the content they want with the device that is appropriate for them at the moment, and there is no end in sight to the invention of context-sensitive devices, from handhelds to wearables and implants. In time, content will cease to be associated with a particular media type.

How could this insight change a culture worker's thinking? We need to invent the smart successor to repurposing—a methodology for creating core content that can be shaped with equal ease and effectiveness for myriad devices and contexts,
including ones that haven't been invented yet.

Here are some design principles that might help.

Think in transmedia terms from the beginning.
Traditional authoring is formal—that is, one thinks first of the form, drama or novel or game, for example—and it is the form that guides the selection and arrangement of materials. *Transmedia authoring is material in nature, that is, it places the emphasis on developing materials that can be select-ed and arranged to produce many different forms.*

Build worlds, not just stories.
At the heart of core content is an environment—one that will support many stories, characters, artifacts, and play patterns. This environment must contain well-envisioned places, and it must obey consistent physical laws. The principal kinds of being who live there must be defined. In the begin-ning, there is a world. For those of you familiar with Smalltalk, this view is similar to the model-view-controller paradigm. *In transmedia terms, the content experiences one can have via various delivery devices (controllers) constitute different views of the same world (model).*

Create a foundational narrative.
This may be a myth or set of stories or a history or chronology. For nonen-tertainment content, the foundational narrative may be a brand identity statement and a set of value propositions. Rob Tow says that *"foundational narratives are the constitutions of new worlds."* There must be procedures for amending the constitution that are sufficiently difficult to enact so that change occurs only occasionally. Even core content authors cannot exercise the divine right of kings. In some ways, the foundational narrative resembles the bible of a TV series, but it serves also to facilitate the contributions of fan (or customer) communities to the evolution of a content world.

Provide for rituals.
Personal rituals such as naming things (cars, folders, pets) and social rituals such as business meetings or parties are familiar patterns of behavior that help us feel at ease. The constitution may call for ritual proclamations or perform-ances that provide means for introducing

new narrative materials into a world. Voting and governing rituals clarify and strengthen community participation. E-commerce sites that do not support the ritual of negotiation over price will be in trouble in cultures where haggling is the rule of the marketplace.

Support community formation. Regular spam emails to people registered on a particular Website does not encourage community formation; rather, worlds should provide affordances for affiliation and communication among people with shared interests or goals. *Community members should be enabled to communicate and interact with one another in as many ways as possible.* Communities cannot exist without boundaries, and so the constitution should also provide means for exclusion.

Give people roles and ways to create personal identities. Active participation keeps a world alive. People want to know how they can interact with a world and what sorts of things they can do. Define specific, appropriate roles; for example, *critic, expert, fan, contributor,* or *customer.* It should be easy for a person to establish a personal identity in the world. Affordances for creating identity will vary depending on whether its function is private or social. People may participate as characters who improvise dramatic action of the world, as in a role-playing game. In that case, characters function as personal identities, whether or not they correspond to the person's identities in real life.

Build scenarios to explore situated contexts. You need to understand the cultural, social, personal, and temporal aspects of all of the ways in which a person may encounter your content. The resilience of a transmedia property can be tested by creating scenarios that source the core content in different situated contexts and through different devices. Scenarios—*plausible little stories about how different people in diverse situations might encounter the world*—can identify both holes and superfluities in the core content.

I've learned some things about business by doing them right,
and some things by really blowing it. If you are the creative lead,
the inventor, or the person with the Big Idea,
these rules of thumb may help you in the business world.

Act like a leader.

Act like a leader. **When I contracted with a nontraditional, woman-dominated development team to create the prototypes for Purple Moon, I tried to gain the approval of my new colleagues through egalitarianism. By the time I came to my senses and started acting like a leader, I saw that my failure to put clear organizational structure in place had allowed dysfunctional social dynamics to grow like weeds. Recovering from the resulting misadventures cost Purple Moon precious months to market.**

Trust yourself.

Trust yourself. **Later in the game, my sense of inferiority in business led me to ignore precious insights and to accede to bad business decisions. Contractors, employees, investors—I was always trying to please someone. Looking back on the experience, I see that I knew much more than I gave myself credit for—and most of the time, my judgment and instincts were right after all. Lack of self-confidence was my greatest enemy.**

Be the vision-keeper. **Only propose what your heart can get behind. If you choose to be a utopian entrepreneur, your vision drives the business. Opening the vision up to revision is a tempting but lethal technique for achieving buy-in. As vision-keeper, your job is to make the vision so clear and compelling that all the players understand it fully and are completely convinced of its value.**

You are not the CEO. **You are probably not the President, either. Unless you have experience as a chief executive, you will be wise to leave that role to somebody who's really good at it. You don't need to be the boss in order to be the creative leader in a company.**

Make sure the CEO has time to run the company. **Purple Moon's CEO had great management skills—but the day-to-day operation suffered because she had to spend so much of her time raising money. Our Chairman was busy with other commitments, and our original CFO was green. When our CEO was on the road, her absence left a management vacuum in our relatively flat organization. Be sure you have a Chairman and other officers who are capable of shouldering a large share of fund-raising activity.**

Insist on being a member of your Board of Directors. **If you're not, you will never know what really happened. As Purple Moon was being shut down, the CEO and I listened in amazement as two of our Board members dispassionately bashed us over the speaker-phone— the conversation had begun as a conference call, and they forgot that we were on the line! I know that many decisions about my company were made through off-the-record conversations among investors. But as a Board member, at least I was able to ask questions (no question is stupid), participate in discussions, raise issues, and vote.**

Your Board must be active business partners. **You will need your Board members to work—really work—for your company. Board meetings are not where you go to make routine updates or manage expectations. Board meetings are where you hunker down and make the most important decisions in your company's life. Your Board members must have energy, experience, skills, wisdom, and mind-share to contribute. For the sake of balance, make sure that at least one member is a noninvestor who is a successful professional in a field relevant to your business.**

Understand the economy of your business. **It's tempting to think of the business plan as a tool for raising enough cash to see the business through to an IPO or acquisition. But a real business plan is not just about money; it's about value. Everything has an economy—even non-profit services and charities. To whom does your product or service have value? Who is willing to pay for that value, and how? Remember that the user may not be the buyer, and that people are less willing than ever to pay for things with their time and attention—a serious weakness of advertising-based business plans.**

Be a realist. **Resist the temptation to create an unrealistic business plan in order to attract investment or to please your Board. Be clear about how long your business will take to be profitable and secure the long-term commitment of your investors. If you don't make your numbers, it's probably better to dial down your burn rate than to borrow money. Every debt your company incurs makes it less attractive to future investors or buyers.**

Avoid an adversarial relationship between Marketing and Product Development. **Institutionalized conflict between marketing and development is a well-established team sport in Silicon Valley, and it is entirely counter-productive. Everyone who works for a company should be on the same side. Using the same research to inform both functions can de-fuse antagonism and increase cooperation. It may seem that consensus-based decision-making empowers everyone, but the converse is more likely true. Over-reliance on**

Be a
realist.

Live
healthy.
work
healthy.

consensus can leave a small company paralyzed. **The absence of clear decision-making processes can channel employees' desires to participate into covert alliances and office politics. Effective organizations have explicit processes for soliciting and expressing employees' opinions. They also assign clear responsibility, authority, and accountability to decision-makers.**

Live healthy; work healthy. **A plan that relies on sustained heroic efforts will damage people and jeopardize the entire enterprise. If they are to be reliably excellent contributors at work, people need relaxation, exercise, sleep, and time for their personal lives. Most of all, you need to apply this rule to yourself. Regardless of the fate of your business, emerging with your health and heart intact will allow you to pursue another**
dream on another day.

And remember:

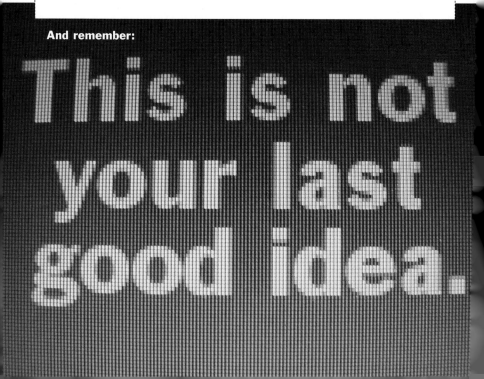

This is not
your last
good idea.

It is all well and good to create these handy heuristics, but we also have to come to grips with the fact that today, content creators are underfunded and under siege because of failing business models. For example, for several years it's been a losing proposition for most content creators to sell their wares to television. Advertising doesn't pay the way. TV companies insist on a piece of merchandising revenue from the content creator in order to put a show on the air. As channels multiply, this situation only gets worse. On the Web, click-through rates on ads continue to plummet, and only a handful of dot-coms are making their way into the black on the basis of advertising revenues or transaction fees.

When business models begin to fail, content creators are likely to take the first hit. Web businesses in particular will allocate more and more of their dwindling resources to propping up the advertising model. Larger providers will engage in a frenzy of consolidations to acquire stockpiles of repurposeable content. Diversity declines as the little guys continue to go out of business. This ugly situation will continue until somebody smart enough to take advantage of the opportunity creates new business models with which content—real, engaging content—can flourish. Again,

BUSINESS INNOVATION
IS AS IMPORTANT AS

TECHNOLOGICAL INVENTION.

We face a crisis in content—who will make it, how will it be paid for, and what will it be worth in a new media world?

Content is inseparable from its economic frame.

We are learning from the failure of advertising that people are less willing than ever to pay with their time. The advertising economy has accustomed us to submitting ourselves and our children to commercial messages in exchange for content that we actually value.

Until recently, this economy of attention
has been invisible—we thought of broadcast television
as providing content for free. It was only when alternatives began to appear that we became aware of the true cost of commercial television, and we saw we might have a choice about how we would pay for TV content. When commercial-free premium channels became available through cable and satellite services, many of us discovered we would rather pay for TV with money than with mind-share.

People appreciate direct value and tend to honor direct economic relationships.

No one likes being the victim of unsolicited advertising;
no one enjoys supporting the middleman who provides no direct value;
no one likes thinking of herself as just a dumb consumer. Teenagers in particular hate being tricked into giving attention to advertising embedded in their media.

And no one likes being interrupted, disrespected, or lied to.

"Better" advertising will provide neither a cultural nor an economic solution. Instead, we might consider the idea of a direct economy for content as a source of new business models.

Direct economies come in many flavors. We can even imagine a direct economy for advertising: request marketing. This model relies on the fact that advertising does have value to people under certain conditions. REQUEST MARKETING provides a means to deliver relevant advertising when—and only when— a person asks for it.

A PEER-TO-PEER ECONOMIC MODEL may work for some kinds of content, as companies like eBay have demonstrated. In this model, the enabling company takes a small percentage of transactions as its revenue. SUBSCRIPTIONS are another form of direct economy. Although subscriptions still have a bad rap on the Web, we often forget the billions of dollars in subscription-based revenue garnered by walled gardens such as AOL and Compuserve. Resistance to subscriptions will decrease as internet access is increasingly provided by cable services, to whom people are already accustomed to paying subscription fees. As with cable TV, people will discover they would rather pay for Web content with money than submit to an endless barrage of advertising that degrades their experience and wastes their time.

The revolution may not be televised, but it will be economic.

Of all the economic models I have encountered, the idea of micropayments seems most promising. Comics guru Scott McCloud does an excellent job of advocating the micropayment model in his book, *Reinventing Comics* (2000), and at ScottMcCloud.com. All it takes is the billing intelligence of a long-distance phone company to give us an infrastructure on the Web that can charge a small fraction of a penny per page view (or some other unit of measure) and send the customer a single monthly bill. Hypertext visionary Ted Nelson once noted that the objection to micropayments by the bit, byte, page or chapter might be valid, but you need to start somewhere. *This is another perfect way for the utopian entrepreneur to prove her design genius by creating a new economic model.* If we wish, we can even decide to devote some micropayments to support the transmedia equivalent of public broadcasting. And then,

I fervently hope, creativity will explode,

people will get direct value, and content creators

can earn an honest living. Such conditions would serve our culture well.

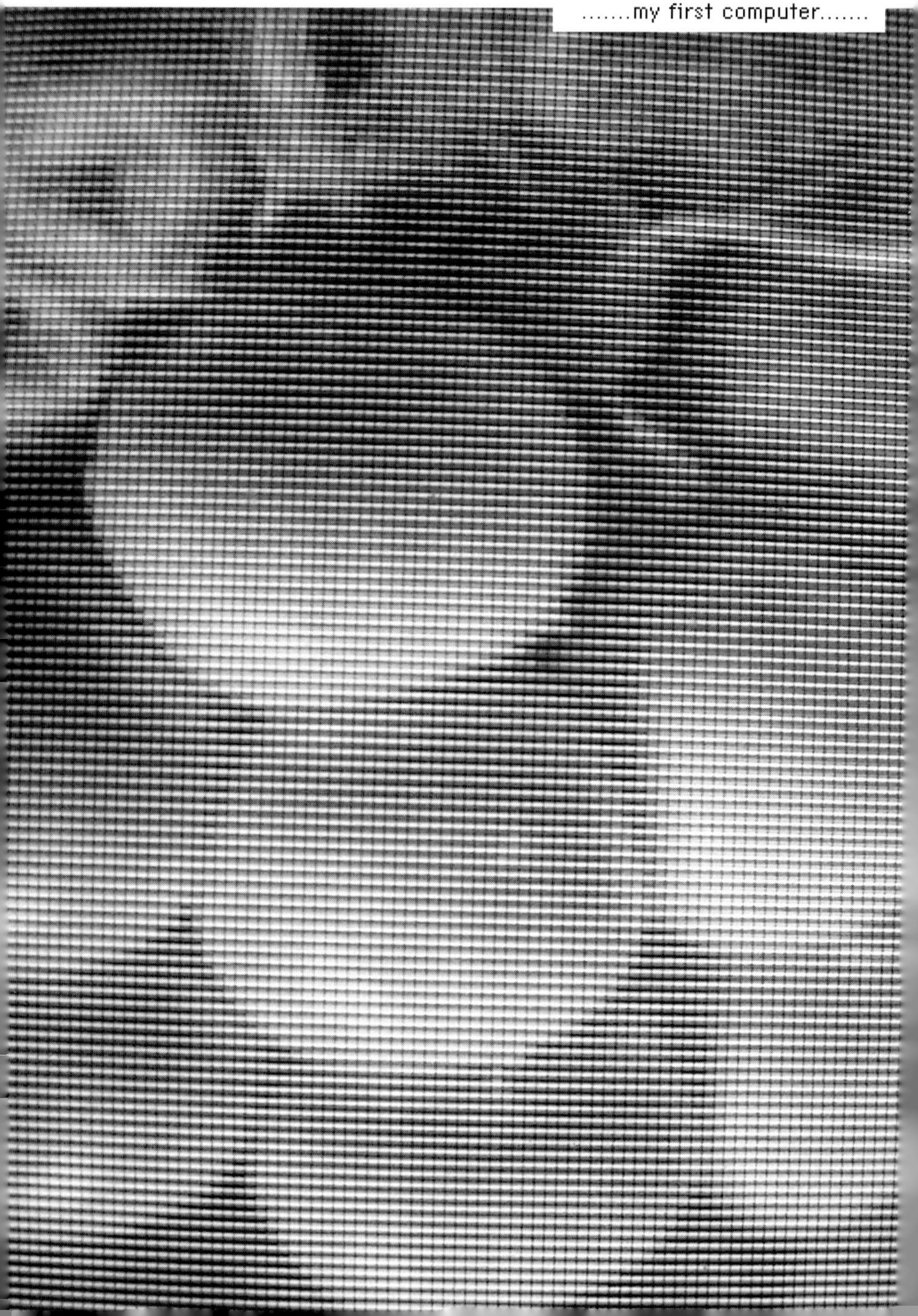

It was Halloween and I was almost twelve. It was a year when extra-big everyday things were the most popular sort of costume—Andy Warhol's influence, I suppose. Perhaps because we lived in Indiana, my mother had the idea of dressing me as an ear of corn. In my grandmother's basement, she fitted me with a chicken-wire frame. She cut armholes with tinsnips and then carefully stapled puffs of yellow fabric to the frame for kernels. She made crisp green taffeta leaves to camouflage my arms, and topped the contraption with gold yarn tassels that tended to flop forward over the tiny eyeholes.

Every year, the little local shopping center sponsored a Halloween costume contest, and the year I was an ear of corn my mother was sure that I would win the grand prize. She had carefully clipped the announcement in the local paper. When we arrived at the shopping center on the evening of the contest, Mother lowered the Ear over my head and took my hand to lead me to the contest tent. The tiny eyeholes gave me tunnel vision. I couldn't bend in any direction, and I could take only small steps without grating my shins on the ends of the chicken wire. We made our way slowly to the tent, a tottering Ear of Corn and a small, purposeful woman.

We arrived at the tent only to find it empty. My mother dug the clipping from her purse. She consulted her watch. It was seven-thirty, we were in the right place at the right time. What had happened? She read that the contest organizer was the manager of the Ace Hardware store at the other end of the mall. She turned and marched me down the sidewalk as fast as I could waddle. When we got to the hardware store I was temporarily blinded by the florescent light pouring into my little eyeholes. My mother dragged me resolutely toward the counter in the back. "What happened to the costume contest?" she demanded.

I could hear the manager's voice, although I couldn't see him. "Aaah, we actually finished early since everyone showed up at seven. We, uh, went ahead."

"How could you do that?" my Mother intoned, her voice rising. "Can't you see that my daughter would have won? And that we were on time? My daughter would have won the prize. What do I tell her now?" I could feel their gaze on me as they contemplated my glorious costume and the disappointment I must be feeling. All the little noises in the store had gone silent. I had the sense that others were watching. I felt that I had become an object of wonder and pity.

The manager hesitated, then proclaimed loudly, taking in the other customers, "I will give your daughter a prize. She is a wonderful Ear of Corn." He led the two of us down an aisle, my leaves sweeping little hardware-store things off the shelves as we passed, and stopped at the small toy section.

The manager picked up what looked like a gray plastic box with the word "Eniac" printed on it.

"It's a computer," he explained. Holding the device directly in front of my eyeholes, he demonstrated its operation. He showed me a small card with a question printed on it—"What is the distance of the earth from the sun?" He inserted the card into the plastic box and turned a crank. A card was ejected from the other end of the device with the number $92,876,479.56$ printed on it. "You see?" he said excitedly. "It can answer questions. All kinds of questions. Here are the questions, right here." He brandished a packet, which presumably contained all of the important questions one might ever want to ask. "All you have to do is feed them into the computer."

I had an epiphany.

For a moment I was transported out of my chickenwire cage,
out of the age of schoolbooks and typewriters,
and into a glorious time when computers
would answer all the really hard questions for us.
Maybe it could even explain to me
what I was doing in the hardware store dressed as an ear of corn.

"Thank you," said Mother, graciously. "It's very nice.
Next year, please run your contest on time."

"I will, Ma'am." The manager shook one of my leaves.
"I'm sorry, honey. You look great.

Enjoy your computer."

Beneath the surface realities of commerce and media, we live in a mytho-
logical field, with a hardwired need and capacity to respond deeply to the
symbols culture provides. Joseph Campbell cautioned that culture fails us
when our symbols are not vitally connected to our lives.

I want to close by thinking about what kind of a cultural symbol the
computer is, asking whether it provides the vital connection to our lives
that keeps our culture well. A culture worker, as we've seen, traffics in both
technology and story, so it's worth wondering,

is the computer
a good mythical character?

The little plastic Eniac that was my first computer contained values.
The computer, the questions, and the answers were a closed system—all a
person got to do was turn the crank. It is time to change that story. The
questions and the answers are human. The computer—well, the computer
ought to be human, too. As human as language. As human as a thumb, a
talisman, a fairy tale, a song.

What is the ethos of the computer—its distinct characteristics, its
moral nature, its guiding principles? It shows up as an innocuous zippy little appliance and a world-dominating soulless megalomaniac, and we recognize it in both roles. In Stanley Kubrick's *2001*, it recites nursery rhymes
without comprehension and locks Dave out of the pod bay, and we recognize it in both actions. In Apple's inaugural ad campaign of 1984, an athlete
hurls a javelin into its big-brother eye and it pops up again as a little box
with a self-effacing smile on its own small screen, and we recognize it in
both disguises.

Although it can speak with
a human voice or display
a human face, we know it is not human.
It is a brain in a box,
without body, soul, intuition,
passion,
or morality. It is the last stop on the road to mind-body dualism.

IT IS A SEVERED HEAD

—severed from the body of what it means to be human. It is also a mega-head, a hypertrophied brain that can grow dangerous if it becomes embodied or self aware. Indeed, it is different from us, but it's also similar enough to us that we think of it, no longer as a machine or a tool, but as an **Other** in relation to the human **Self**. It functions in our cultural mythology to express dualities—mind and body, other and self, logic and compassion, reason and intuition, technology and nature. Yes, we made the computer, but in its role as a cultural symbol, the computer also defines us.

And so, you gotta ask yourself, what kind of future has this character in it?

And if you don't particularly like the answer, then you have to turn the question around—what kind of character can act out a future that we would like to live in?

Cultural narratives coax technologies into being, and vice versa. That's why the Apollo space program owes a considerable debt to H. G. Wells. It's also why Ronald Reagan's pet defense technology was nicknamed "Star Wars." It's why slick commercials of beautifully dressed housewives effortlessly operating gleaming chrome-trimmed home appliances lured women out of the post-World War II workplace. It's why that young pilot in the Gulf War compared his bombing mission to a videogame. It's why computer software and technology invented for and by **culture workers will change both the technology and the ethos of computing.**

Culture and technology exist in dynamic reciprocal relationship. Culture comprehends technology through the means of narratives or myths, and those narratives influence the future shape and purposes of technology. The culture-technology circuit is at the heart of cultural evolution.

As we become more capable of radically altering the conditions affecting our biological survival through technological means, cultural evolution becomes the primary factor in our ability to survive. The stories that we tell quite literally influence our fate as a species.

In his book *Wonderful Life: The Burgess Shale and the Nature of History* (1989), Harvard biologist Stephen Jay Gould observes that the two traits that distinguish human beings from their forebears are *abstract reasoning and representational art*. Tool use was not sufficient to lead to us; other tool-using humanoid species died out. Gould points out that humanity is "an improbable and fragile entity, fortunately successful after precarious beginnings as a small population in Africa, not the predictable end result of a global tendency." We are unlikely, not a done deal; nor would evolution predict that we are to be the progenitors of an even more "intelligent" species than ourselves. The story of evolution is neither the unfolding of a divine plan nor the inevitable march of sentience toward more and more spectacular manifestations; rather, extinction is the rule. We are much more likely to die out than to transform into a self-aware, infinitely smart, infinitely wise collective being shrouded in white light, the internet notwithstanding. As far as evolutionary history would predict, the same traits which got us into this mess are going to have to be the ones that get us out of it —namely, *abstract reasoning and representational art*. Computers, of course, *are extremely good at augmenting both activities. Coincidence?*

When I look into the future,
I can scare myself out of optimism quite easily, much less utopianism.

I see a world where dominator politics prevail, where human rights abuses multiply in direct relation to increasing poverty and overpopulation. I see world religions in a state of rigor mortis, with a death grip on science, art, and the exchange of ideas. I see the ecology of the Alaskan Arctic devoured by petro-gluttony and the forests of Indonesia in flames. Worst of all, I see a world where people can't talk to each other in any meaningful way. Global networking will be a tool of business communication, consumerism, propaganda, banal conversations, and mindless entertainment. We will have forgotten how to tell stories or to hear them. The majority of the world's population will be very young people without extended families or intact cultures, with fanatical allegiances to dead religions or live dictatorships. We have what Jonas Salk called a "wisdom deficit"—fewer elders and even fewer people who listen to them.

But I started off by claiming a mantle of utopian entrepreneurship.
WE CAN MANIFEST
A DIFFERENT FUTURE,

AND WE MUST.

Throughout this book, I've maintained that one way to accomplish this is to activate the culture-technology circuit, to make the computer a character worthy of myth.

It is not enough to simply call for this and then hope for the best; we need interventions at the level of popular culture. Culture workers at their best make just such conscious interventions—mindfully creating technologies that cause us to produce new myths, and mindfully making art that influences the shape of technology.

Today, humanistic culture work is possible and it is necessary. The Enlightenment humanists' core values and methods were at odds with both the institutions of power and the "popular culture" or street wisdom of the time. By bravely deploying their contemporary mass media, the Encyclopaedists brought about profound changes in institutions, cultural practices, arts, sciences, and philosophy, which continue to frame our lives today. Every one of us has the opportunity to

employ similar methods and to express similar

values.

I wish us all a great deal of courage, self- discipline, and clear-eyed hope.

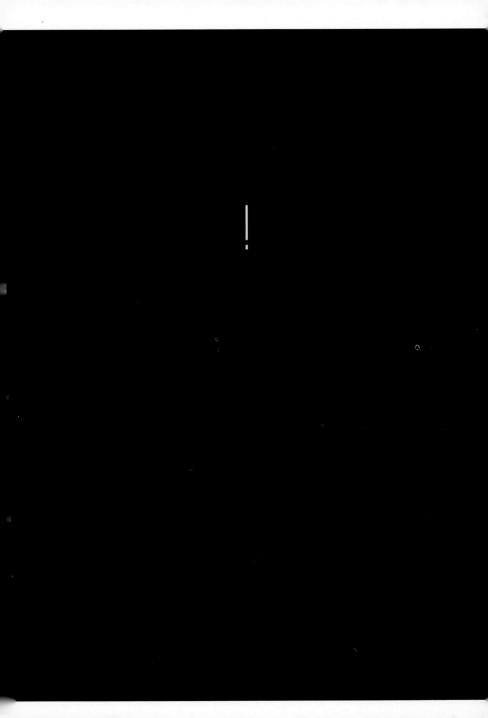

Endtroduction.

The book you have in your hands was defiantly created to be just that, a thing to be held. We've come through a period drunk with the promise of electronic networks, disembodied flows, and the irtualization of anything that can't be nailed down. But such intoxication doesn't last forever, and we move from a moment when information wanted to be free to one in which knowledge strives to find form. That's why *Utopian Entrepreneur* is so emphatically an object.
Its physical presence—the specifics of its form—matter.
Utopian Entrepreneur is the first in an ongoing series of Mediawork pamphlets, which pair writers who matter with today's most innovative designers to create compact, intellectually sophisticated, visually compelling texts. Their designation as pamphlets counters the bloat that affects so much contemporary theory and criticism, ensuring concision and demanding rigor from authors and designers alike.

Brenda Laurel, digital diva and friend, is ideally suited to kick off this series. I offer her my thanks for taking a leap into the unknown. Laurel has long been a key figure in the digital arena, author of the perennial best-seller *Computers as Theatre* and editor of *The Art of Human-Computer Interface Design*.

As *Utopian Entrepreneur* so wittily describes, Laurel was centrally involved in four of the digital economy's big booms: gaming in the late 1970s, Virtual Reality in the late 1980s, CD-ROM publishing in the early 1990s, and the dot.com explosion just now waning. In *Utopian Entrepreneur* she reflects upon her experiences and filters them through scrims of critical theory, millennial feminism, and business narrative. Denise Gonzales Crisp has done far more than bring form to Laurel's words; she shaped the look and feel of the *Mediawork* pamphlets series as a whole. A self-proclaimed "decorationalist," she makes work that embraces pleasure and plentitude. Rather than a rote illustration of content, she develops a retinal language, melding concern for meaning with a reflexive design intelligence.

Further *Mediawork* pamphlets will explore art, literature, design, music, and architecture in the context of emergent technologies and rapid economic and social change. I sometimes think of *Mediawork* pamphlets as "'zines for grown-ups," commingling word and image, enabling text to thrive in an increasingly visual culture. But the aims of the series extend beyond creating theoretical fetish objects. *Mediawork* pamphlets transform private theory into public discourse. By private theory I mean those ideas that circulate within the hermetically sealed spheres of academia and the techno-culture. The pamphlets select texts from these discourses, distill insights and interventions from them, design a supportive visual context, and launch these hybrids out into a greater public. The *Mediawork* pamphlets series is not intended to "replace" other forms of discussion—from books to journals to listservs to Web 'zines—but rather to create a new category of public visual intellectuals.

We drew from a range of inspirations, I'll mention just two here. The first was the 1960s collaboration between media theorist Marshall McLuhan and designer Quentin Fiore that resulted in the marvelous little mind bombs, *The Medium is the Massage* and *War and Peace in the Global Village*. In the early 1980s, Sylvère Lotringer's Semiotext(e) published Jean Baudrillard's *Simulations*, that small black volume which ignited a fury of theoretical activity. Lotringer began with industrial design: Semiotext(e) books were sized to fit directly into the vest pocket of a leather bomber jacket. I'm not sure that *Mediawork* pamphlets have that specific

a destination, but we were thinking about those sling
packs, messenger bags, and attachés that both men
and women now shoulder to hold their pens, pads, pagers,
phones, PDAs, and, of course, laptop computers. These
pamphlets are the perfect size and weight to toss into
one of these bags or slip into an outer pocket. I hope
people page through *Utopian Entrepreneur* while they
wait for their laptops to boot up. Interstitial times
demand interstitial literature.

Making theoretical fetish objects requires support
and funding. Major ongoing funding for *Mediawork*
pamphlets comes from the Rockefeller Foundation. The
first three pamphlets have been supported by a start-up
grant from Jeffrey and Catharine Soros. Additional
funding has been provided by the Office of the President,
Art Center College of Design. I would like to thank Doug
Sery at The MIT Press, who has been unstinting in his
support of the series and unflagging in his friendship.
Personal thanks to Jeffrey Soros who acted as a venture
philanthropist, to Art Center's President Richard
Koshalek who put the institution's weight behind the

project, and to Joan Shigekawa from the Rockefeller Foundation for ensuring its long term viability. I'm lucky enough to have Brenda Laurel and Denise Gonzales Crisp as colleagues on the faculty of Art Center's graduate program in Media Design, so I knew they couldn't bail out when the going got rough. This institutional safeguard wasn't necessary, though, as their brilliance and enthusiasm never waned. As always, thanks to my wife, Susan Kandel, and our children, Kyra and Maud, for everything else.

Peter Lunenfeld, Editorial Director

Designer's Note.

Giving form to another's words is challenging, particularly when the words are as direct from heart to pen as those of Brenda Laurel. Add to this the unlikely chance that a designer could match—let alone manifest—Peter Lunenfeld's energy and aspiration for the project, then the task becomes even more daunting. But it was exactly this immediacy and exuberance that helped determine my approach.

I was attracted to the Mediawork pamphlets concept from the outset. The pocketable insight of a small book parallels my interest in speaking to individual readers directly through design. And though *Utopian Entrepreneur* parades here a bit as fetish object, hopefully its form sidesteps spectacle and invites spirited interaction.

For the record, this work deliberately references two other small (in size) books in which form plays a significant role: John Berger's *Ways of Seeing*, and Marshall McLuhan's *The Medium is the Massage*, designed by Quentin Fiore.

I thank Peter for thinking to include me, and Richard Koshalek for backing me in this inaugural effort. Thanks also to Stuart Frolick and my associates at the Art Center Design Office, whose support on this and all my work adds up to more than my abilities merit; and to my husband, John Hartzog, who stubbornly insisted that I invest in the tools that led me to discover the simple joys of digi-stitching.

Denise Gonzales Crisp

Author's Acknowledgements.

I am indebted to my editor and colleague Peter
Lunenfeld for making me write this book and to
Denise Gonzales Crisp for making it beautiful.

By my best reckoning, over a hundred people
worked on Purple Moon. The project was made possible
by David Liddle and was supported by Noel Hirst, Bonnie
Johnson and other colleagues at Interval Research.
Christopher Ireland and Davis Masten of Cheskin
Research masterminded the study of gender and play,
mentored me in business, and helped me navigate every
obstacle. Kristee Rosendahl designed the Website and
all the real stuff with creativity and class. Pamela Dell
created familiar, quirky, amazingly relevant characters
and situations for our world. Storyteller and lifelong
friend Lucinda Delorimier gave every path a heart.
Lili Cunningham presided over production with endless
energy and grace. Kathleen Watson managed marketing
with integrity and respect for girls. And Nancy Deyo led

the company like the hero she is. Thanks and praise to
these and all the other artists, designers, writers, and
professionals for their extraordinary effort, talent, and
commitment.

I am most grateful to Rob Tow for our ongoing
spiritual and intellectual partnership. To the girls—
Hilary, Brooke, and Suz—thanks for making Purple Moon a
family business, and for inspiring my work at every turn.

Brenda Laurel

The MIT Press
Cambridge, Massachusetts
London, England

Utopian Entrepreneur
by Brenda Laurel

A Mediawork Pamphlet
http://mitpress.mit.edu/mediawork

This book was set in Adobe Univers, Adobe Franklin Gothic, Adobe Sassoon Primary,
Hoefler Engraved, and Emigre Universal Eight & Nineteen.
Photo illustrations © 2001 Denise Gonzales Crisp.

Printed and bound in the United States of America.

Library of Congress Control Number: 2001092089
ISBN 0-262-62153-3